THE ADVENTURES OF TOM SAWYER

THE GREENHAVEN PRESS
Literary Companion
TO AMERICAN LITERATURE

THE ADVENTURES OF TOM SAWYER

Katie de Koster, *Book Editor*

David L. Bender, *Publisher*
Bruno Leone, *Executive Editor*
Bonnie Szumski, *Series Editor*

Greenhaven Press, Inc., San Diego, CA

Every effort has been made to trace the owners of copy-
righted material. The articles in this volume may have
been edited for content, length, and/or reading level. The
titles have been changed to enhance the editorial purpose.
Those interested in locating the original source will find
the complete citation on the first page of each article.

Library of Congress Cataloging-in-Publication Data

Readings on The adventures of Tom Sawyer / Katie
    de Koster, book editor.
        p.   cm. — (The Greenhaven Press literary
    companion to American literature)
    Includes bibliographical references and index.
    ISBN 1-56510-845-0 (lib : alk. paper). —
ISBN 1-56510-844-2 (pbk. : alk. paper)
    1. Twain, Mark, 1835–1910. Adventures of Tom
Sawyer. 2. Adventure Stories, American–History and
criticism. 3. Boys in literature. I. de Koster, Katie,
1948–   . II. Series.
PS1306.R43   1999
813'.4—dc21   98-26113
                                                             CIP

Cover photo: The Bettmann Archive

Copyright ©1999 by Greenhaven Press, Inc.
PO Box 289009
San Diego, CA 92198-9009
Printed in the U.S.A.

" I conceive that the right way to write a story for boys is to write so that it will not only interest boys but strongly interest any man who has ever been a boy. That immensely enlarges the audience. "

Mark Twain, letter to Fred J. Hall,
August 19, 1892

Contents

Chapter 1: The Art of the Novelist: Creating *Tom Sawyer*

Chapter 2: The Individual and the Community in Tom Sawyer's World

FOREWORD

"'Tis the good reader that
makes the good book."

Ralph Waldo Emerson

The story's bare facts are simple: The captain, an old and scarred seafarer, walks with a peg leg made of whale ivory. He relentlessly drives his crew to hunt the world's oceans for the great white whale that crippled him. After a long search, the ship encounters the whale and a fierce battle ensues. Finally the captain drives his harpoon into the whale, but the harpoon line catches the captain about the neck and drags him to his death.

A simple story, a straightforward plot—yet, since the 1851 publication of Herman Melville's *Moby-Dick*, readers and critics have found many meanings in the struggle between Captain Ahab and the whale. To some, the novel is a cautionary tale that depicts how Ahab's obsession with revenge leads to his insanity and death. Others believe that the whale represents the unknowable secrets of the universe and that Ahab is a tragic hero who dares to challenge fate by attempting to discover this knowledge. Perhaps Melville intended Ahab as a criticism of Americans' tendency to become involved in well-intentioned but irrational causes. Or did Melville model Ahab after himself, letting his fictional character express his anger at what he perceived as a cruel and distant god?

Although literary critics disagree over the meaning of *Moby-Dick*, readers do not need to choose one particular interpretation in order to gain an understanding of Melville's novel. Instead, by examining various analyses, they can gain numerous insights into the issues that lie under the surface of the basic plot. Studying the writings of literary critics can also aid readers in making their own assessments of *Moby-Dick* and other literary works and in developing analytical thinking skills.

The Greenhaven Literary Companion Series was created with these goals in mind. Designed for young adults, this unique anthology series provides an engaging and comprehensive introduction to literary analysis and criticism. The essays included in the Literary Companion Series are chosen for their accessibility to a young adult audience and are expertly edited in consideration of both the reading and comprehension levels of this audience. In addition, each essay is introduced by a concise summation that presents the contributing writer's main themes and insights. Every anthology in the Literary Companion Series contains a varied selection of critical essays that cover a wide time span and express diverse views. Wherever possible, primary sources are represented through excerpts from authors' notebooks, letters, and journals and through contemporary criticism.

Each title in the Literary Companion Series pays careful consideration to the historical context of the particular author or literary work. In-depth biographies and detailed chronologies reveal important aspects of authors' lives and emphasize the historical events and social milieu that influenced their writings. To facilitate further research, every anthology includes primary and secondary source bibliographies of articles and/or books selected for their suitability for young adults. These engaging features make the Greenhaven Literary Companion series ideal for introducing students to literary analysis in the classroom or as a library resource for young adults researching the world's great authors and literature.

Exceptional in its focus on young adults, the Greenhaven Literary Companion Series strives to present literary criticism in a compelling and accessible format. Every title in the series is intended to spark readers' interest in leading American and world authors, to help them broaden their understanding of literature, and to encourage them to formulate their own analyses of the literary works that they read. It is the editors' hope that young adult readers will find these anthologies to be true companions in their study of literature.

INTRODUCTION

Images from *Tom Sawyer* spring readily to mind: the children in the cave, the discovery of pirate gold, and especially the fence-whitewashing incident. These episodic and often fantastic adventures of children in pre–Civil War America have led many critics to consider *Tom Sawyer* a children's book. But while it is indeed a "boy book"—a book *about* boys—it was originally intended for an adult audience.

Before *The Adventures of Tom Sawyer*, Mark Twain had always written for adults. *Roughing It*, a book that relates his Western adventures, was published in 1872. *Tom Sawyer*, published four years later, was originally cast in much the same mold: a semiautobiographical reminiscence, this time about his childhood in Hannibal, Missouri. As he wrote, Twain aimed the work at his contemporaries, the same audience who had enjoyed his humorous take on life in his other writings. After he had finished it, however, both his wife, Livy, and his good friend William Dean Howells, the editor of *Atlantic Monthly,* persuaded Twain to present the novel as a children's book.

Howells reviewed the book for his magazine, emphasizing the good character of Tom ("an ordinary boy on the moral side"), the reform of Huck (although he did admit that "in his promised reform his identity is respected: he will lead a decent life in order that he may one day be thought worthy to become a member of that gang of robbers which Tom is to organize"), and the "instructive" nature of Twain's setting ("which gives incomparably the best picture of life in that region as yet known to fiction"). Downplaying the revolutionary aspects of Twain's vision, Howells set the book firmly in the genre of children's literature of the day, although he did admit to the "grownup reader's satisfaction in the amusing and exciting story."

A century later, it is impossible to tell whether Livy and Howells gave Twain good advice in urging him to market the novel as a book for children. Literature for young people at the time was usually instructional and uplifting, tales of good children who succeed by acting in ways approved by adults and of bad children who come to grief by ignoring the rules. Twain had taken the traditional boy book and stood it on its head, showing his disdain for "good" children in his portrayal of Sid, the pompous tattletale, and his clear approval of Tom and Huck, who are indulged by society even while they flout its rules. This endorsement of the boys' shocking behavior led some who considered themselves moral guardians to condemn the work, much to Twain's delight, since the controversy sold books. But the controversy distracted readers from exploring the depth of the novel, which speaks to readers on many levels and has something to offer even the most mature and sophisticated adult.

The book can be enjoyed by children, of course, as humor, fantasy, and adventure. It takes a somewhat older reader to relate to Tom's loss of innocence, as envisioned by Twain: not the kind of loss that comes with learning about Santa Claus, but the kind that comes from realizing that evil exists and has power in the world. Tom's struggles with his fear and his conscience when the wrong man is accused of murder mark his emergence from childhood and the beginnings of acceptance of grown-up responsibility.

Adults who read the book are often surprised to find an entirely different perspective. Many view *Tom Sawyer* as a study about society's role in "civilizing" its children. Twain brought a refreshing stance to the often repressive attitudes of his day, creating a picture of society that indulged youthful high jinks yet managed to guide its children without entirely squashing their high spirits. It is an attitude that seems so modern today that it may be difficult to realize how revolutionary—even heretical—it seemed to many readers a century ago.

It may take a certain maturity to discern in *Tom Sawyer* the theme that Twain would advocate for the rest of his life: namely, that "adult" rules and the insistence that children abandon their innocence and adopt civilization's "grown-up" values are destructive. The bitterness that would mark Twain's later writings is not yet evident at this early stage in his career; there is merely a hint in the joyously colorful portrayal of Tom in the early chapters that fades to a vaguely disappointed picture of the young man as he begins to fit himself into a respectable mold. This theme may best be discerned by adults looking back over their own lives and examining choices made and compromises accepted or rejected.

The decision to market the novel as a children's book may well have been the best way for Twain to sell more books—and selling books was always a high priority for him. But that long-ago decision should not keep readers of all ages from indulging in the pleasures of *The Adventures of Tom Sawyer.*

Mark Twain: A Biography

A word of warning is in order for those who wish to know the truth about Mark Twain: He wrote autobiographical fiction and fictional autobiography—and he is the primary source of information about his own life. The life of Mark Twain is a story told by Samuel Langhorne Clemens, and his accounts, dates, and embellishments are all, so to speak, subject to verification and clarification. When Twain was writing his autobiography, he made it plain: "I don't believe these details are right but I don't care a rap. They will do just as well as the facts."

Fortunately for those who value facts over a more artistic truth, Twain wrote prolifically in notebooks and in letters to family and friends, and many of these writings have survived. Researchers have painstakingly studied these private manuscripts for indications of "what really happened," combining them with reminiscences of his family, friends, and business associates to set the record straight.

Florida, Missouri

> I was born the 30th of November, 1835, in the almost invisible village of Florida, Monroe County, Missouri. . . . The village contained a hundred people and I increased the population by 1 per cent. It is more than many of the best men in history could have done for a town. It may not be modest in me to refer to this but it is true.

The baby who would grow up to write the preceding in *The Autobiography of Mark Twain* was christened Samuel Langhorne Clemens when he was born in that tiny hamlet in Missouri. His parents, John Marshall and Jane Lampton Clemens, both originally of Virginia families, had met in Kentucky. When they married in Lexington in 1823, Jane was twenty and John twenty-four or -five, and "neither of them had an overplus of property. She brought him two or three negroes but nothing else, I think," reported Sam. Although they were not wealthy, they were considered "gentry." The couple moved to Tennessee, where they tried to make a living in several small towns, but a steady decline in their fortunes led them to look for better opportunities farther west. The family sold nearly all they had (except for thousands of acres of undeveloped Tennessee land and their one remaining slave) and began the hard journey to Florida, Missouri, in the spring of 1835.

The two-room frame house with a lean-to kitchen in Florida must have been crowded; when they moved in, the Clemens family already included Orion (born 1825; the family pronounced his name with the accent on the first syllable), Pamela (born 1827), Margaret (1830), and Benjamin (1832). There would be one more son after Sam—Henry, born in 1838. (Pamela remembered another son, Pleasants Hannibal, who had died in Tennessee at the age of three months.)

Florida was a town with prospects. Founded on the Salt River, surrounded by rich land, already the location of flour mills, a sawmill, and distilleries, it seemed to need only vision and development to make it a bustling commercial center. But the U.S. economy suffered a crash in 1837, and the envisioned improvements for Florida never happened. John Clemens was always a better visionary than businessman; his own business—a store—was failing. In the fall of 1839, soon after Sam's sister Margaret died from "bilious fever," John traded his holdings in Florida for land and buildings in nearby Hannibal, Missouri, on the Mississippi River, and moved his household again.

HANNIBAL, MISSOURI

Although the family's fortunes continued to decline, the next few years gave young Sam the childhood he would later chronicle (with a few changes, of course) in *The Adventures of Tom Sawyer* and *The Adventures of Huckleberry Finn*. The Clemenses had moved to Missouri to be near Jane's sister, Patsy, and her family. Patsy's husband, John Quarles, was a successful farmer, respected and popular, and—unlike Sam's rather austere father—genial and generously good-natured. "I have not come across a better man than he was," wrote Sam many years later. Sam began spending the summers at the Quarles farm, and his memories of that time as recorded in his autobiography are splendid:

> It was a heavenly place for a boy, that farm of my uncle John's. The house was a double log one, with a spacious floor (roofed in) connecting it with the kitchen. In the summer the table was set in the middle of that shady and breezy floor, and the sumptuous meals—well, it makes me cry to think of them. Fried chicken, roast pig; wild and tame turkeys, ducks and geese;

venison just killed; squirrels, rabbits, pheasants, partridges, prairie-chickens; biscuits, hot batter cakes, hot buckwheat cakes, hot "wheat bread," hot rolls, hot corn pone; fresh corn boiled on the ear, succotash, butter-beans, string-beans, tomatoes, peas, Irish potatoes, sweet potatoes; buttermilk, sweet milk, "clabber"; watermelons, muskmelons, cantaloupes—all fresh from the garden; apple pie, peach pie, pumpkin pie, apple dumplings, peach cobbler—I can't remember the rest.

The farm, with its orchards, barns, stables, wandering brook with forbidden (and therefore irresistible) swimming pools, and slave quarters (where Sam became friends with several of the slaves), played a role in the later literature of Mark Twain: "In *Huck Finn* and in *Tom Sawyer, Detective*, I moved [the farm] down to Arkansas," he recalled. "It was all of six hundred miles but it was no trouble; it was not a very large farm—five hundred acres, perhaps—but I could have done it if it had been twice as large."

The generous summer lifestyle, which probably began when Sam was seven or eight, may have contributed to his survival. He had been a sickly child and said he "lived mainly on allopathic medicines during the first seven years" of his life. As Twain biographer John Lauber points out, "Merely to live was an accomplishment for such a child, demonstrating unexpected toughness at a time when, according to a Hannibal paper, 'one quarter of the children born die before they are one year old; one half die before they are twenty-one.'" The Clemenses had already lost Margaret at the age of nine and the infant Pleasants Hannibal; Benjamin would die when he was ten, in 1842.

But Sam seemed to survive against all odds, even when he made the odds longer against himself. In 1845 Hannibal was hit with an epidemic of measles that killed many of its children. "There was a funeral almost daily and the mothers of the town were nearly demented with fright," he recalled. Jane Clemens went to extraordinary lengths to keep Pamela, Henry, and Sam away from contagion, with the result that Sam, now about the age at which Margaret and Benjamin died, constantly feared he had caught the deadly disease. He finally decided he could live in suspense no longer, and snuck into bed with a seriously ill friend, Will Bowen. It took two tries—he was caught the first time and hustled out of the sickroom—but he managed to get "a good case of measles" that took him "within a shade of death's door."

An energetic and mischievous boy, Sam attended school reluctantly. He excelled in the weekly competitive spelling bees, but did not otherwise distinguish himself, especially not in deportment, his brother Henry's forte. He later wrote, "My mother had a good deal of trouble with me but I think she enjoyed it. She had none at all with my brother Henry, who was two years younger than I, and I think that the unbroken monotony of his goodness and truthfulness and obedience would have been a burden to her but for the relief and variety which I furnished in the other direction."

A DARKER SIDE OF HANNIBAL

Although Missouri would officially side with the North during the Civil War (1861–1865), it had entered the Union as a slave state under the terms of the Missouri Compromise of 1820 (an attempt to prevent the issue of slavery from tearing the nation apart). Sam Clemens thus grew up with slaves. His family's decline could be charted by the sale of their slaves over the years; finally, having none of their own, they rented slaves by the year from neighbors. He later recalled:

> In my schoolboy days I had no aversion to slavery. I was not aware that there was anything wrong with it. No one arraigned it in my hearing; the local papers said nothing against it; the local pulpit taught us that God approved it, that it was a holy thing and that the doubter need only look in the Bible if he wished to settle his mind—and then the texts were read aloud to us to make the matter sure.

Sam Clemens would be an adult before he came to an understanding of slavery as "a bald, grotesque and unwarrantable usurpation." But he did relate to the slaves he knew as people: "All the negroes were friends of ours, and with those of our own age we were in effect comrades. I say in effect, using the phrase as a modification. We were comrades and yet not comrades; color and condition interposed a subtle line which both parties were conscious of and which rendered complete fusion impossible."

The subtle line maintained by a slaveholding society remained, but his empathy for his slave friends was awakened by his mother:

> We had a little slave boy whom we had hired from some one, there in Hannibal. He was from the eastern shore of Maryland and had been brought away from his family and his friends halfway across the American continent and sold. He was a cheery spirit, innocent and gentle, and the noisiest creature that ever was, perhaps. All day long he was singing, whistling, yelling, whooping, laughing—it was maddening, devastating, unendurable. At last, one day, I lost all my temper and went raging to my mother and said Sandy had been singing for an

hour without a single break and I couldn't stand it and *wouldn't* she please shut him up. The tears came into her eyes and her lip trembled and she said something like this:

"Poor thing, when he sings it shows that he is not remembering and that comforts me; but when he is still I am afraid he is thinking and I cannot bear it. He will never see his mother again; if he can sing I must not hinder it, but be thankful for it. If you were older you would understand me; then that friendless child's noise would make you glad."

It was a simple speech and made up of small words but it went home, and Sandy's noise was not a trouble to me any more.

In Hannibal, separating and selling the members of a slave family "was a thing not well liked by the people and so it was not often done, except in the settling of estates," he remembered. But the rare sight of a dozen black women and men chained together, awaiting shipment to the southern slave market, left him with a memory of "the saddest faces I have ever seen." Another memory was seeing a Negro man killed by a white man "for a trifling little offence"; everyone seemed indifferent to the slave's fate, sympathizing only with the owner who had lost valuable property.

Violent death was a danger not only for slaves in that nearly frontier town. Sam suffered nightmares after witnessing several other tragedies: the shooting of an old man "in the main street at noonday" by a wealthy businessman who just walked away, unmolested, after taking this revenge for a slight; the stabbing of a young California emigrant by a drunken comrade; attempted murder by two brothers who held down their uncle and tried to shoot him with a revolver that would not fire; the death of another California emigrant who threatened a widow and her daughter and was answered by a chestful of slugs from an old musket.

THE DEPTHS OF POVERTY

Meanwhile, John Clemens's lifelong pattern of steady decline in fortunes, interrupted by brief flashes of prosperity, continued. John Lauber writes that "things went badly for the Clemenses in Hannibal. Creditors pressed them hard, they moved frequently, there was a sheriff's sale in 1843 and another ordered in December 1846—but the sheriff found nothing left to seize. . . . Orion was apprenticed to a printer in St. Louis—much against his will, for he felt that he was a gentleman's son and deserved a profession." In 1846 the Clemenses were reduced to sharing quarters with another family, for whom Jane cooked.

According to the family tradition, the 1846 calamity was the result of John's "going security for" (cosigning) a large note for a man named Ira Stout, who then declared bankruptcy and left the Clemenses ruined by the liability to pay the entire note. Their fortunes were about to turn around again the next year, they believed, when the ultimate disaster hit:

> When my father died, in 1847, the disaster happened—as is the customary way with such things—just at the very moment when our fortunes had changed and we were about to be comfortable once more after several years of grinding poverty and privation. . . . My father had just been elected clerk of the Surrogate Court. . . . He went to Palmyra, the county-seat, to be sworn in about the end of February. In returning home horseback twelve miles[,] a storm of sleet and rain assailed him and he arrived at the house in a half-frozen condition. Pleurisy followed and he died on the 24th of March.
>
> Thus our splendid new fortune was snatched from us and we were in the depths of poverty again.

Perhaps John Clemens's most valuable legacy to his son was his precise and careful use of the English language. John and Sam also shared a strong intellect and a deep integrity; dreams of wealth and a desire for success; independent thinking, shaded by a strain of pessimism; involvement in the affairs of their communities (which, for Sam, would become the world community); and an abiding sense of justice.

Samuel Charles Webster, a grandson of Sam's sister Pamela, wrote that "Mark Twain inherited his humor, his temperament, and his red hair from his mother's side. His accuracy in workmanship he got from his father. His accuracy in facts he never got from anybody."

"NEWSPAPER COLLEGE"

Although he later said he had been taken from school immediately upon his father's death, recent research has shown that Sam continued to attend school at least part-time for two more years. But in his fourteenth year, he was apprenticed to Joseph Ament, publisher of the weekly Hannibal *Courier.* He was to board with his master, learn the printing trade, and receive two suits of clothing a year (he got just one—Ament's oversized castoff). He soon graduated to setting type, and to making mischief with his fellows.

In the nineteenth century, printing was "the poor man's college." Newspapers were consciously "literary," offering poems and essays from both classical and contemporary authors, and liberally borrowing the best pieces from one another. Although Sam had been an unenthusiastic schoolboy, he now became an eager reader, and began the self-education that would continue throughout his life.

After the discovery of gold in California in 1848, the editor of the Hannibal *Journal* joined the gold rush, and Orion decided the time was ripe to start his own paper in Hannibal. He began the weekly *Western Union,* and offered his brother Sam $3.50 a week plus board to join him. As that was $3.50 more than the *Courier* paid, Sam accepted.

Like their father, Orion was a lousy businessman, and the promised pay failed to materialize more often than not. But Orion did offer Sam something the *Courier* had not: an opportunity to get his own work into print.

THE FIRST NEWSPAPER WRITINGS

Sam's first published work was "A Gallant Fireman," a one-paragraph anecdote in the January 16, 1851, *Western Union,* describing the antics of the paper's "printer's devil," Jim Wolf, when a fire broke out in the grocery store next door to the newspaper office. In May of the following year, Sam's work gained a much larger audience. "The Dandy Frightening the Squatter," a humorous tale, appeared in the Boston *Carpet-Bag* on May 1, 1852. Exactly a week later, the Philadelphia *American Courier* printed Sam's description of the town he would later make famous as Tom Sawyer and Huck Finn's St. Petersburg: "Hannibal, Missouri."

By fall 1852, Sam was on a roll. "A Family Muss," a report on a drunken man's assault on family and friends livened by the use of a comic Irish dialect, appeared with Sam's pseudonymous by-line "W. Epaminondas Adrastus Perkins" on September 9 in the Hannibal *Journal.* (Orion had purchased a second paper and merged them; the publication was now known by this name.) The following week, on September 16, Sam entered his first journalistic feud, with the editor of the rival Hannibal *Tri-Weekly,* who had responded sarcastically to one of Orion's editorials.

By May 1853 the *Journal* was struggling to survive, and Sam decided to try to do better elsewhere. In late May or early June he set out for New York (although he told his family he was headed for St. Louis, to keep them from worrying—or perhaps from trying to stop him).

BREAKING AWAY

An accomplished typesetter could find work in almost any town. Sam did stop in St. Louis for a few weeks to earn money for the rest of his journey; then he headed for New York City. Arriving in late August 1853, he was soon employed by a printing house and writing long letters home. His family had apparently heard lurid tales of what could happen to a young man alone in the big city; in one of his letters, Sam wrote: "You ask me where I spend my evenings. Where would you suppose with a free printer's library containing more than 4,000 volumes within a quarter of a mile of me, and nobody at home to talk to?" (Free public libraries were still relatively rare; most libraries were founded for a defined group of people—printers, sailors, merchants—or were subscription libraries, charging a fee.)

The free reading was about all Sam could afford. His pay was poor, so in October he moved to Philadelphia, where he worked for the *Inquirer.* His hours were odd but the pay was better, allowing him to enjoy his spare time seeing the sights, and even take a quick trip to Washington, D.C. But the novelty of the city was wearing off.

In late summer 1854, he briefly rejoined his brothers Orion and Henry and his mother, who were now living in Muscatine, Iowa, then returned to St. Louis for a few months, working as a printer but wishing he could be a riverboat pilot. When Orion married and moved to Keokuk, Iowa, to open a printing shop with Henry, Sam joined them for about a year and a half. He was reading voraciously but apparently not writing for publication, although he discovered he had a talent for public speaking, a talent that would save him financially more than once.

On November 1, 1876, in response to a letter from an old friend, J.H. Burrough, Sam recalled himself at that time:

> As you describe me I can picture myself as I was 22 years ago. The portrait is correct. You think I have grown some; upon my word there was room for it. You have described a callow fool, a self-sufficient ass, a mere human tumble-bug, stern in air, heaving at his bit of dung and imagining he is re-molding the world and is entirely capable of doing it right. Ignorance, intolerance, egotism, self-assertion, opaque perception, dense and pitiful chuckle-headedness—and an almost pathetic unconsciousness of it all. That is what I was at 19–20.

MAKING HIS FORTUNE, PART I

As usual, Orion's business was doing poorly. He made Sam a partner, who would share the "profits" instead of drawing his promised five-dollar weekly salary. Sam could tell this was no way to get ahead. Having failed to persuade a wealthy relative to help him finance his dream of becoming a riverboat pilot, Sam now had a new scheme for making his fortune: "I had been reading Lieutenant Herndon's account of his explorations of the Amazon and had been mightily attracted by what he said of coca," he reported in his autobiography. "I made up my mind that I would go to the head-waters of the Amazon and collect coca and trade in it and make a fortune." (The addictive and destructive powers of cocaine were little recognized then.)

Sam spent the winter of 1856–1857 in Cincinnati, Ohio, working at the printing office of Wrightson and Company to earn money for his passage to South America. Perhaps the most noteworthy aspect of this period was a friendship he struck up with a fellow boarder, a Scotsman named Macfarlane. Little is known about him—not his occupation, not even his first name—but he said he was a self-educated man, and he had developed his own philosophy, which impressed the young typesetter who was half his age. Sam spent many evenings with Macfarlane that winter, listening to him explain his reasoning. His theory of evolution, propounded some fifteen years before Charles Darwin published *The Descent of Man*, made a particularly strong impact on Sam:

> Macfarlane considered that the animal life in the world was developed in the course of eons of time from a few microscopic seed germs, or perhaps one microscopic seed germ, . . . and that this development was progressive upon an ascending scale toward ultimate perfection until man was reached; and that then the progressive scheme broke pitifully down and went to wreck and ruin!
>
> He said that man's heart was the only bad heart in the animal kingdom; that man was the only animal capable of feeling malice, envy, vindictiveness, revengefulness, hatred, selfishness . . . the sole animal in whom was developed the base instinct called *patriotism*, the sole animal that robs, persecutes, oppresses and kills members of his own immediate tribe, the sole animal that steals and enslaves the members of any *tribe.*

Whether Macfarlane planted seeds that blossomed later in Mark Twain or simply found a soul already compatible with his philosophy, those who read the writings of Mark Twain's last years will recognize in them the same bitter pessimism expressed in the Scot's ideas.

By springtime, Sam had saved enough to pay his way to New Orleans on the steamer *Paul Jones.* He planned to set sail for the Amazon from that port, but on the way south he met one of the boat's pilots, Horace Bixby, whom he soon persuaded to help him become a riverboat pilot. Bixby agreed to teach Sam the Mississippi River from St. Louis to New Orleans for five hundred dollars—one hundred dollars in advance. Sam borrowed the advance from William Moffett, who had married his sister Pamela, and began to learn the snags, curves, and hidden obstacles of the great river.

Mark Twain wrote of his life on the Mississippi, with a certain amount of literary license, in the book called, appropriately, *Life on the Mississippi.* Being a pilot was much more than adventure and travel. Riverboat pilots were respected, almost revered. Once the boat left shore, they were in supreme command, not even subject to orders from the captain. Piloting required intense attention to details, which had to be committed to memory—an admirable trait for an author-to-be to develop. The job was lucrative: A master pilot could expect the same income as the vice president of the United States. The financial security, and the confidence that came from the sense of command, eventually led Sam to take over the role of head of the family from the feckless Orion. It was now Sam who found employment for their brother Henry.

Sam was a cub pilot on the *Pennsylvania* in June 1858, working under William Brown, master pilot and petty tyrant. Henry was working as third (or mud) clerk on the same boat when Brown accused him of insubordination and attacked him with a lump of coal. Sam sprang to his brother's defense, the only recorded time he resorted to physical violence.

As it turned out, this episode may have saved Sam's life, but it led to a lifelong feeling of guilt. Because of the altercation Sam left the ship in New Orleans, but Henry stayed aboard. At six o'-clock on the morning of June 13, 1858, the *Pennsylvania*'s four boilers exploded. The boat had just won a race with a rival steamer and was preparing to race another; the boilers (one of which was known to leak badly) had been fired up to the limit. At least two hundred people died immediately; many others—including Henry—later succumbed to their injuries. Sam, who was traveling north as a passenger on the *A.T. Lacey*, arrived in time to be with his brother, who lived for six days. He blamed himself for Henry's having been on the *Pennsylvania.* The guilt he felt was only made worse by those who congratulated him on his luck for not having been aboard, as scheduled.

The accident did not drive Sam from the river, although he did take a month off, another lucky break during which he missed an epidemic of yellow fever in New Orleans. On April 5, 1859, he received his pilot's license.

A respected gentleman now, he decided that chewing tobacco was no longer appropriate for his new position in life, and he quit for good. He began to dress with style. He apparently made friends readily, and there was no shortage of young women to dance with at fancy parties. The slightly built man whose head seemed a little too large for his body, with red curly hair, blue-green eyes, and "a Roman nose, which greatly improves the beauty of his features" (according to his daughter Susy, in the biography she wrote when she was thirteen), had found a career he planned to follow until the end of his days.

The Civil War intervened.

THE CIVIL WAR

In his autobiography, Mark Twain did not dwell on the war:

> I was in New Orleans when Louisiana went out of the Union, January 26, 1861, and I started North the next day. Every day on the trip a blockade was closed by the boat [it was the last one allowed to go through], and the batteries at Jefferson Barracks (below St. Louis) fired two shots through the chimneys the last night of the voyage. In June I joined the Confederates in Ralls County, Missouri, as a second lieutenant under General Tom Harris and came near having the distinction of being captured by Colonel Ulysses S. Grant. I resigned after two weeks' service in the field, explaining that I was "incapacitated by fatigue" through persistent retreating.

This offhand treatment does not reveal the difficulties Sam had in deciding which side to take in this conflict of brother against brother. Missouri was a border state; although it stayed in the Union, many of its citizens fought for the Confederacy. The Clemens family had owned slaves, and Sam had grown up with "the Peculiar Institution." Orion, however, was a staunch abolitionist.

"The Private History of a Campaign That Failed," written by Mark Twain in 1885, tells more about the choice Sam Clemens made. (Although the details may be fictionalized, family members' accounts and the reminiscences of other participants verify that the overall picture was accurate.) It is a story that recalls the differences between Tom Sawyer and Huckleberry Finn. Sam and several of his friends from Hannibal got together one night and formed a military company. They dubbed themselves the Marion Rangers and made almost everyone an officer; Sam was second lieutenant. Setting out on an "expedition" in a Tom Sawyer spirit of horseplay and fun, they basically went on a prolonged campout, playing at military drills on occasion. When rumor of an approaching enemy force reached them, the council of war (everyone in the troop) agreed that the main concern was that they not retreat *toward* the enemy.

A losing battle with a farmer's dogs was followed by several scares about Union troops searching for Confederates to hang. The frequent rumors soon lost their force, however, so that one night, after another report of an approaching enemy, it was a surprise when a lone horseman did appear. Sam fired on him; when no other troops appeared, the Rangers crept out of hiding to approach their foe.

> When we got to him the moon revealed him distinctly. He was lying on his back, with his arms abroad; his mouth was open and his chest heaving with long gasps, and his white shirt-front was all splashed with blood. The thought shot through me that I was a murderer; that I had killed a man—a man who had never done me any harm. That was the coldest sensation that ever went through my marrow. I was down by him in a moment, helplessly stroking his forehead; and I would have given anything then—my own life freely—to make him again what he had been five minutes before. And all the boys seemed to be feeling in the same way. . . . They had forgotten all about the enemy; they thought only of this one forlorn unit of the foe. . . . He muttered and mumbled like a dreamer in his sleep, about his wife and child; and I thought with a new despair, "This thing that I have done does not end with him; it falls upon them too, and they never did me any harm, any more than he."
>
> In a little while the man was dead. He was killed in war; killed in fair and legitimate war; killed in battle, as you may say; and yet he was as sincerely mourned by the opposing force as if he had been their brother. . . . It soon came out that mine was not the only shot fired; there were five others,—a division of the guilt which was a grateful relief to me.

In his notes for *The Adventures of Huckleberry Finn,* Twain wrote, "A sound heart and a deformed conscience [prevailing but misguided social dictates] come into collision, and conscience suffers defeat." Like Tom Sawyer, who in *Huckleberry Finn* indulged in fantasy games to "free" Jim even though he knew he was unnecessarily risking Jim's life, the Marion Rangers were playing at the adventure of war. Like Huck, who defied his conscience and indulged his heart to help Jim escape slavery, Sam finally refused to play that popular game.

Some of the Marion Rangers went on to become efficient, effective soldiers, but Sam had had enough of war. After falling back with his fellows a few more times, he (along with about half the troop) set out for home.

HEADING WEST

Although his sympathies were on the Union side, Orion no more wished to fight than Sam did. Orion had campaigned for

Abraham Lincoln for president, and an old friend of his, Edward Bates, was Lincoln's attorney general. This fortunate combination resulted in Orion's appointment as secretary of the Nevada Territory, which had been created on February 28, 1861, from land taken from Mexico. Like California with its gold, Nevada with its Comstock lode of silver (discovered in June 1859) was considered vital to the Union, so officials were dispatched to the new territory quickly. Orion could not afford the fare, but Sam (who had been supporting Orion and his family since he began earning a pilot's wages) had an idea: He would become the unofficial secretary to the new secretary and pay the way for both of them. (Orion's wife, Mollie, and daughter, Jennie, were to remain in Iowa temporarily.) The brothers went up the Missouri River to St. Joseph and, on July 26, 1861, they were off by stagecoach to Carson City. They reached that new capital of the Nevada Territory on August 14, after a journey evocatively described in Twain's *Roughing It.*

MAKING HIS FORTUNE, PART II

Before long Sam ventured out of Carson City. He and a friend staked a timber claim in the nearby countryside (the silver mines needed timber to shore up tunnels), but their campfire got out of control and burned down their prospective profits. He turned to mining for a while, the prospect of unlimited riches being irresistible, but found it a hard life, again with no profit. He was still writing letters home, some of which were published in a Keokuk paper, and he began sending humorous letters (signed "Josh") to the Virginia City *Territorial Enterprise,* Nevada's leading newspaper. Just as he was beginning to feel desperate about his financial situation, the *Enterprise* offered him a job as a full-time reporter for twenty-five dollars a week. It was not the millions he had been planning to make, but he accepted and set out for Virginia City.

With its new millionaires, its rough population struggling to become the *next* millionaires, and its frontier conditions, Virginia City seemed a model of the wild and woolly West. In its anything-goes atmosphere, Sam's extravagant style found plenty of room to grow. For the first time, writing was a vocation for Sam. Here he found colleagues whose examples helped develop his talent, especially the *Enterprise*'s Dan De Quille (called "Dandy Quille" by his friends, his real name was William Wright) and Clement T. Rice of the rival Virginia City *Union,* whom Sam dubbed "the Unreliable" and with whom he carried on a wild and friendly literary rivalry.

It was here, on February 2, 1863, that Mark Twain was born. This new pseudonym was clearly taken from Sam's steamboat days. "Mark twain" is the cry of the leadsman announcing that the boat is in two fathoms (twelve feet—the minimum for safety) of water.

Sam—now becoming known as Mark Twain—had restless feet, so it is unlikely that he would have remained in Nevada for long. By the spring of 1864, he wrote in *Roughing It,* "I wanted to see San Francisco. I wanted to go somewhere. I wanted—I did not know what I wanted. I had spring fever and wanted a change, principally, no doubt." Perhaps his spring fever made him more reckless in writing than usual; he managed to annoy and insult quite a few people, among them James Laird, publisher of the *Union.* Egged on by colleagues at their respective papers, Laird and Twain soon found themselves committed to a duel. Dueling was illegal, and some of those he had insulted were threatening to bring other charges against him. On May 29 prudence (and restlessness) prevailed; he took the stagecoach to San Francisco.

CALIFORNIA

Mark Twain had been a good-sized frog in a smallish pond in Nevada and, judging from his reports of his activities there, the *Enterprise* did not overwork him. In these respects California was a letdown. He complained, "After leaving Nevada I was a reporter on the *Morning Call* of San Francisco. I was more than that—I was the reporter. There was no other. There was enough work for one and a little over, but not enough for two—according to Mr. Barnes's idea, and he was the proprietor and therefore better situated to know about it than other people." The workday began at nine a.m. with an hour at the police court and ended at eleven at night after visits to "the six theaters, one after the other: seven nights in the week, three hundred and sixty-five nights in the year. We remained in each of those places five minutes," he said, and then tried "to find something to say about those performances which we had not said a couple of hundred times before."

Although he was not signing his pieces for the *Call,* he was also writing bylined contributions as Mark Twain for the San Francisco *Californian.* The *Californian* had a knowing, sophisticated tone, and Twain's writing was becoming more consistently satirical and less crude. When he left the *Call,* he had much less money but more time to meet his fellow writers at the *Californian,* including Bret Harte, who thought

Twain's work was comparable to the best of Charles Dickens's sketches. In his connection with Harte and the other writers for the *Californian*, Twain began to see himself as an author rather than a journalist.

Finding himself somewhat at odds with the local authorities (he had posted bail for a friend who then skipped town), Twain went with a friend to an old mining camp on Jackass Hill in Tuolumne, California. To pass the time in the frequently bad weather, Twain began keeping a notebook, making notes on local characters and on the stories they told. One of those stories, with a few Twain embellishments, would later become "The Celebrated Jumping Frog of Calaveras County."

On February 20, 1865, Twain headed out of camp and back toward San Francisco on foot, arriving on February 26. Orion had lost his position in Nevada (from an overabundance of integrity, according to his brother). Will Moffett, their sister Pamela's husband, died that year, leaving her with two children. Thus Twain's self-imposed family responsibilities made his poverty seem even more desperate. He had once told Orion that he would never return home until he had made his fortune; it seemed that would never happen. He considered going back to the river as a military pilot. But even as he was touching bottom, his efforts were slowly beginning to pay off. East Coast journals picked up his writings from western papers, and began to notice this bright new humorist called Mark Twain. In September, the New York *Round Table* called him "the foremost among the merry gentlemen of the California press"; in November, the New York *Weekly Review*, a prestigious journal, said he was "one of the cleverest of the San Francisco writers." These responses heartened the humorist, and he threw himself into his work once again, writing daily letters for the Virginia City *Enterprise* and reviews for the San Francisco *Chronicle*, making enough to begin to get out of debt.

Artemus Ward, a famous western humorist he had met in Nevada, asked Twain for a story for his new book. Twain sent along the story of "Jim Smiley and His Jumping Frog" (Celebrated in a later title as being from Calaveras County). It arrived too late for inclusion in the book, so Ward sent it to the New York *Saturday Press*. Its appearance in that paper's issue of November 18, 1865, wrote the San Francisco *Alta California*'s eastern correspondent, "set all New York in a roar." Widely reprinted, it made its author a minor national celebrity.

Tired of San Francisco and heartened by his growing reputation on the East Coast, Twain began planning his escape. He would write a book; he would collaborate with Bret Harte on one or another joint project; . . . he would become a travel correspondent.

In January 1866 he had been invited to join a select group of passengers on the steamer *Ajax*'s first voyage to the Sandwich Islands, as Hawaii was then called. He had declined, but soon regretted having done so, and persuaded the Sacramento *Union* to send him on the *Ajax*'s March 7 voyage to Honolulu, promising to send them "twenty or thirty letters" at twenty dollars apiece. He spent four months in the islands, writing informative, humorous, picturesque letters for the *Union*'s readers. He gave himself a fictional companion, Mr. Brown, to provide a vulgar counterpart to the genteel observations of Mark Twain—making Twain a fictional character, too.

Returning to San Francisco on August 13, he determined to head east in order to take advantage of the favorable press he was getting. But, though his finances had stabilized (and the Civil War was over), he could not afford passage to the other side of the continent. Thomas McGuire, a friend who owned several theaters, advised him: "Now was the time to make my fortune—strike while the iron was hot—break into the lecture field. I did it." His first San Francisco lecture, based on his tour of the Sandwich Islands, was a smashing success: Not only did the audience love him, but he netted nearly three months' salary for ninety minutes on the stage. He had found the medium that would, time and again, help him dig out from financial woes.

After a triumphal tour of California and Nevada towns, followed by a "farewell" tour in various venues in and around San Francisco, Twain finally had enough money and confidence to return to his family with pride intact. The *Alta California* proudly claimed him as its travel correspondent, who would tour the world and write about it for its readers. On December 15, 1866, he left for New York on the steamer *America.*

MAKING HIS FORTUNE, PART III

Although he was not comfortable with the "frenzied energy" of New York, he found an old California acquaintance, Charles Webb, to publish his first book, *The Celebrated Jumping Frog of Calaveras County and Other Sketches.* Then, after less than six months in New York, on June 8, 1867, he embarked on the first pleasure cruise to sail from an American port, a five-month voyage to the Mediterranean and the Holy Land on the

Quaker City, an adventure whose stories would be told in his book *The Innocents Abroad.*

On this voyage he met Charley Langdon, who showed him a picture of his sister. As Twain later wrote, "I saw her first in the form of an ivory miniature in her brother Charley's stateroom in the steamer *Quaker City* in the Bay of Smyrna, in the summer of 1867, when she was in her twenty-second year. I saw her in the flesh for the first time in New York in the following December." It had taken just that one look at her portrait, Twain said, for him to fall in love with Olivia (Livy) Langdon, daughter of a wealthy coal magnate of Elmira, New York. They were married on February 2, 1870.

By all accounts—those of their intimate friends as well as their own—the two were extremely happy with each other. It was a marriage of contrasts, and they delighted in their differences. Livy called her husband "Youth," recognizing his eternally young nature. She tried to dust him off and make him presentable, and he enjoyed her efforts to do so. He could exasperate her sense of propriety on occasion, but having her as a balance in his life seemed to help him curb (or at least keep private) many of the rash eruptions that had in the past made moving on to another place so frequently a wise decision.

The Langdons' wedding gift to the couple (a complete surprise to their new son-in-law) was a large house, fully furnished and staffed, in Buffalo, New York, where Twain had purchased a one-third share in the Buffalo *Express.* (Jervis Langdon, Livy's father, had advanced him the twenty-five-thousand-dollar purchase price.) The income from Livy's funds would be about forty thousand dollars a year; along with Twain's income, which was growing respectably, the newlyweds were able to live very handsomely.

But while they were happy in each other, their marriage withstood griefs and tragedies almost from the beginning. Jervis Langdon, Livy's beloved father, died of cancer just months after the wedding. Livy, who had spent weeks nursing him, suffered a nervous collapse when he died. She nearly miscarried in October; the baby, a son named Langdon, born on November 7, was frail, sickly, and at least a month premature. He died on June 2, 1872.

Buffalo was not proving a happy home, so the Clemenses sold the house and moved to Hartford, Connecticut. Their second child, Olivia Susan (Susy), was born there on March 19, 1872, followed by Clara (June 8, 1874) and Jean (July 26, 1880).

MAKING HIS FORTUNE, PART IV

The quarter-century after his marriage was a prolific period for Mark Twain. He coauthored with Charles Dudley Warner the book that would give the period its name: *The Gilded Age.* Several books of sketches were interspersed among *Tom Sawyer, A Tramp Abroad, The Prince and the Pauper,* and *A Connecticut Yankee in King Arthur's Court.* When Twain revisited his old haunts for *Life on the Mississippi,* he also found the settings and the memories for what is generally considered his greatest book—although *Huckleberry Finn* was originally just, as the subtitle has it, *Tom Sawyer's Comrade.*

But books were not Twain's only plan for profit. He was an inventor, and was perennially interested in new technology. Unfortunately, he seemed to have inherited the Clemens style of investment: buy high, sell low. He was an easy touch for almost any inventor with a new way to make things work.

One such inventor was James W. Paige, creator of a new typesetting machine. Twain felt confident in assessing the value of the new contraption, since he had been a typesetter, but it was to prove a catastrophic investment. By 1885, he had poured $190,000 into the machine and its inventor.

While he was spending himself into a hole with the typesetter, another investment, Webster & Company publishing house, was costing considerably more than it made—a grave annoyance, since it was counted on to provide income by publishing Twain's work. Along with other bad investments and a financial downturn that wiped out Livy's yearly income from coal stocks, Mark Twain was eventually brought to the point of bankruptcy. Ironically—since his father had been left holding the bag by a bankrupt man—he did not take advantage of the bankruptcy laws that would have allowed him to pay his creditors pennies on the dollar. In July 1895, at the age of fifty-nine, Mark Twain embarked on a world lecture tour; it took him five years to make enough money to repay all his creditors in full.

A DARKER SIDE OF MARK TWAIN

Many critics and biographers have speculated on the cause of Mark Twain's increasingly bitter pessimism in the last decade or so of his life. Although he lived very well in some years, he never was able to feel secure, and he had the Clemens dreams of great wealth. The Tennessee land bought by John Clemens gradually changed hands in transactions that seemed to bring no profit to the family; once Orion scuttled a potentially lucrative sale of part of it because the buyer wanted to plant vineyards there, and that day Orion was a teetotaler. (An untimely new dedication to abstinence from alcohol was also blamed for helping him lose his position in Nevada.) The legacy of land, which John Clemens had confidently expected would make his children wealthy, was instead a curse to Mark Twain:

> With the very kindest of intentions in the world toward us he laid the heavy curse of prospective wealth upon our shoulders. He went to his grave in the full belief that he had done us a kindness. It was a woeful mistake but fortunately he never knew it. . . .
>
> It kept us hoping and hoping during forty years and forsook us at last. It put our energies to sleep and made visionaries of us— dreamers and indolent. We were always going to be rich next year—no occasion to work. It is good to begin life poor; it is good to begin life rich—these are wholesome; but to begin it poor and *prospectively* rich! The man who has not experienced it cannot imagine the curse of it.

Twain had expected to make millions from the Paige type-setter; instead, it helped bankrupt him while he supported its inventor for years. Paige, like Orion, seemed to have a penchant for snatching defeat from the jaws of victory: At least once when the machine seemed to be working well and customers were ready to buy, he decided it must have another embellishment—which never worked.

Twain's bitterness was always entwined with a sense of guilt he could occasionally shake but never completely escape. The Calvinist beliefs of his family and boyhood neighbors—he was raised a Presbyterian—were harsh indictments of sinful man. Although he did not subscribe to the religion of his family, its stern pronouncements delivered while he was young had a strong effect in nurturing his perpetual sense of guilt. He blamed himself for the deaths of his brother Henry, for whom he had found employment; his son, Langdon, whom he had taken for a carriage ride on a cold day; his daughter Susy, who became ill in Connecticut while he and Livy were in Europe (trying to recoup their fortune) and died before they could reach her. He does not seem to have blamed himself for Livy's death—she had been a near-invalid for years before he met her. But the fact that during the many months of her final illness his presence was considered so disturbing that he was not allowed to see her at all for weeks at a time, and only for a few minutes when he was allowed into the sickroom, could not have made a guilt-prone man happy.

A free spirit who disliked authority, he nevertheless accepted the burden of responsibility for his mother, brothers, and sister, supporting them more or less consistently throughout his life. That sense of responsibility made his bankruptcy and its disruptive effects on their lives as well as on his wife and daughters' lives even more crushing a blow. On their silver wedding anniversary, after twenty-five years of marriage, he had nothing to offer Livy but a silver five-franc piece. The bankruptcy, of course, would have threatened the confidence of most people; Twain felt special anger because he believed that many people—inventors and publishers headed the list—had been cheating or otherwise taking advantage of him.

The theft of his works by foreign publishers fed his bitterness. He often had to go to England to attend the publication of his books, since an author had to be in the country at the time of publication in order to receive any copyright protection. Nevertheless, many publishers around the world made money selling the works of Mark Twain without paying him a penny in royalties. (He fought for copyright reform in the United States to prevent similar unfairness for foreign authors; he hoped, of course, that the law would become international.)

He had traveled the world and found much to disturb him in the global community as well as in the personal one. He found war abhorrent, tyranny unforgivable, imperialism unjustified. The more he saw of the world, the more the pessimistic philosophizing of the Scotsman Macfarlane seemed borne out. And in his role as an international celebrity, he saw more of the world's problems—and frauds—than most of his fellows did, because people frequently asked for his support for one cause or another, presenting their pleas with the direst evidence of need.

Mark Twain had seen plenty of death all his life, but as he grew older, so did his friends and family. Jane Clemens died in 1890; so did Livy's mother. Pamela's son-in-law, Charles L. Webster (who had run the Webster publishing house) died in 1891. Pamela died in 1894, as did Orion's wife, Mollie. Susy died in 1896. Orion died in 1897. Livy died in 1904, and his life was thrown out of balance forever. Pamela's son, Samuel (named after his uncle), died in 1908. In September 1909 Clara married and moved to Europe, and Twain settled down with his third daughter, Jean, in Redding, Connecticut. On Christmas Eve, Jean suffered an epileptic seizure and drowned in her bath.

Mark Twain's frequent bouts of pessimism do not seem to present an unsolvable mystery.

HALLEY'S COMET

Although much has been made of Twain's pessimism, his dark view of human nature in his later years, there was still evidence of sanguine Sam. His writings tended to be dark, but his sense of humor was irrepressible. He was still "Youth," and still loved cats and children. He corresponded with and occasionally entertained a coterie of girls, whom he called his "angelfish." He enjoyed their fresh views on life, their innocence, their sense of fun, and they brought back to him his happy days with his own young daughters. He was not perpetually miserable, but he was tired and his life was running out.

When Sam was born in 1835, Halley's comet was visible on its regular return visit toward the sun. He had often said he expected to die when the comet made its next appearance—in 1910. In 1909 he told his official biographer, Albert Bigelow Paine:

> I came in with Halley's comet in 1835. It is coming again next year, and I expect to go out with it. It will be the greatest disappointment in my life if I don't go out with Halley's comet. The Almighty has said, no doubt: "Now here are these two unaccountable freaks; they came in together, they must go out together."

On April 20, Halley's comet reached its perihelion—its closest approach to the sun—and then began its journey back out into the solar system. On April 21, 1910, at about midday he told his daughter Clara, "Goodbye dear, if we meet," and then fell into a doze. Around sunset, he died.

CHAPTER 1

The Art of the Novelist: Creating *Tom Sawyer*

READINGS ON
THE ADVENTURES
OF TOM SAWYER

Why *Tom Sawyer* Is an American Masterpiece

Henry Seidel Canby

Mark Twain transformed the experiences of his boyhood into art, creating a masterpiece that reflects American themes of freedom and westward movement, declares Henry Seidel Canby. Twain's exaggerations and inventiveness enrich the tale of the young hero, who has a deep and interesting personality not seen before in literature about children. Canby, editor of the *Saturday Review of Literature* and a former professor at Yale University, is a respected critic.

Sam Clemens was born in the struggling log village of Florida, Missouri, on November 30, 1835. Until he was four years old, and was taken to live on the great river at Hannibal, his childhood was normal for thousands upon thousands of children whose parents or grandparents had crossed the Alleghenies before the Civil War and were settling the great central land which stretched to the Indian country beyond the Mississippi. This central land, the Middle West, was of the same general pattern from the western slopes of the mountains through Ohio and Kentucky and Tennessee on to the prairies and the plains. It had been the greatest hardwood forest in the world, and still enclosed among settled farms and hacked-out clearings great tracts of wilderness. Even near the villages it was wild, but not savage, not dangerous. It was conquered land, conquered from the Indians, the French, the British, but more importantly, conquered from nature. Back from the village settlements and the country and river towns, life and its human abodes were still crude and raw. If these backwoods settlers were not still pioneers, they lived like them, and on slight excuse would move on West again. But this frontier life was hearty in spite of malaria and typhoid, agreeably free, and rough, if sometimes disagreeably tough. Sam's father's family had brought a tradition of literate, courteous Virginia with them into Tennessee. His mother had been a lively Kentucky girl, famous for her dancing, at home in the new frontier culture as her husband never became. Both, like at least half of their neighbors wherever they settled, were still mobile; seeking some western star of prosperity. The family barouche, a relic of Virginia grandeur, was soon left behind on the way. At last, on the great river, they came, not to prosperity, but to rest. Mobility was in the blood of this Westward-turning strain. Mobility was in the stories Sam heard as a child. For a while in this early mid-century, the tempo of change in the middle land was rapid beyond precedent in American history. A single generation passed from trader with the Indians, to pioneer hunter, to frontier clearings, and then to the log villages and rough farm houses where Sam Clemens' family birthed their children, and finally to the little towns which were already "civilized" in what was to be an American pattern for a century. And each stage had left its survivors who kept the morals and the manners of the past in a changed environment. When the boy Sam went back for the summer to Uncle John Quarles' farm at Florida, fifty miles from the river, he lived in much the same backwoods culture across which his father and family and a slave had moved from log village to log village in the great forest.

The past was present even for a boy. Drunken Pap Finn, Huck's father, complained with entire justice that the so-called march of civilization had reduced a free hunter and fisher living in a land of plenty to poverty and drink—made a poor-white of him. Injun Joe, the half-breed, Tom Sawyer's boyhood terror, recalled the fur traders and their squaws of a generation earlier. It was river pirates preying upon immigrants who hid the treasure that made Tom and Huck rich....

Behind all frontier mobility of the center land were two dynamic motives. The first was a desire for freedom from castes and classes, from cramped land and forbidden opportunity—freedom (the Negroes always excepted) to be self-willed, to rise in the social scale, and almost equally to degenerate. Now that we are emerging from the false absolutes of the economic interpretation of history, the craving for freedom in this broad sense is seen to be a fundamental shaper of American society. [Walt] Whitman understood its power, and based much of his romantically optimistic but psychologically sound poetry upon an idealization of the shiploads of immigrants he watched disembarking in the harbor of New York on their way to the West. *Tom Sawyer* and *Huckleberry Finn* are boys' epics of freedom. . . .

TOM AND HUCK . . . AND SAM AND MARK

I am writing in this section a literary biography of Mark Twain the writer, not a complete study of Samuel Langhorne Clemens. For Sam Clemens' boyhood in Hannibal, I do not propose to compete with Mark himself. The substantial accuracy of the background of *The Adventures of Tom Sawyer* and *Adventures of Huckleberry Finn* has never been questioned. They are full of "stretchers," which was what Huck called the exaggeration and romanticizing of Tom. And it is not surprising to learn that Becky Thatcher was not too much like her original in the village, and that the major events of the stories were a reminiscent dream of what might very well have happened. The important question seems to be the relation of Tom and Huck in the books written about them to the highly personal imagination of Mark Twain. What will become clearer as we go on is that vital aspects of Sam Clemens and his boyhood are lifted into symbolism and then made brilliantly concrete in these books. If you wish to find out what Sam was like and what he did or wished to do you must read them. They are much the best history of his actual life in Hannibal, even if they are full of "stretchers." And you must read them if you are to understand the later Sam who, as Mark Twain, turned this "boy-life" into an art which has deeply influenced the imagination of millions of readers. . . .

To begin with, *Tom Sawyer* is a small-town book and *Huckleberry Finn* is a great-river book. . . . The focus of *Tom Sawyer* is school, home, and the adventures of two boys exploring the night life of St. Petersburg and the romantic freedom of the islands. Its emphasis is upon freedom as the Westward-turning American experienced it in youth. The focus of *Huckleberry Finn* is always the river, and its theme also is freedom, but in a dramatic counterpoint where Huck, who has run away himself to be free, encounters a runaway slave for whom freedom is a crime against the morals of Hannibal. *Tom Sawyer* is a miniature, sharp and vivid; *Huckleberry Finn* is a mural with an epic rhythm.

Tom Sawyer is of course Sam Clemens, but only one aspect

of a self-conflicting personality, which was dual throughout his life. Tom's adventures are the stretched wish-fulfillments of a romantic boy. He dreamed of robbers and pirates and made his companions believe in them. When the wish, as often with a boy, tangled with reality, Sam gave to Tom the adventures that such a boy would like to have experienced himself, yet kept them real and familiar. Injun Joe belongs to the dream world of a boy, but he came true in Hannibal, and the Tom in Sam knew how to handle him. All his life, as we shall see, Mark Twain was Tom when he was not someone else; particularly in his books, but often in his own life. It was the insatiable ego of Tom, always craving a show-off, that invented the Yankee and sent him back into the Age of Chivalry to overthrow the knights by lasso and six-shooter [in *A Connecticut Yankee in King Arthur's Court*]. Sam was the tender-minded Tom who left his pirate friends on the island to steal across the river and kiss Aunt Polly in her sleep. It was the romantic Tom in Mark who discovered with such a shock that the God in whom Aunt Polly believed was not a humanitarian, nor even moral. It was the Tom in Mark who turned romantic pessimist in the end, thinking that he was hard as nails. William James saw Twain only when in 1892 they lived near each other in Italy, but it was enough for that great psychologist to see that he did not belong among the tough-minded in his famous categories.

"A fine soft-fibered little fellow," so he described him in a letter to Josiah Royce, "with the perversest twang and drawl, but very human and good. I should think one might get very fond of him."

Most of all, Tom Sawyer had the quality which was to make Mark Twain's easier success, and, carried to an extreme, some of his worst failures. He was immensely inventive, whether in plots, like the murder story of Injun Joe, or in such absurdities as the rescue of the Negro Jim after he was known to be free already. It was the flow of invented exaggeration which made Mark's really very informational lectures a triumph of splendid clowning, and got him his first pseudo-literary reputation in the East. Invention is the indispensable gift of a triumphant storyteller. . . . Mark invented or experienced his own stories, and told them on a springboard—from which sooner or later he was sure to turn a double somersault in the air, to the delight of the vulgar and the dismay of the judicious.

Twain's beloved daughter Susy remarks that "the difference between papa and mama is, that mama loves morals and papa loves cats." Susy's intuitions were more accurate than her childish vocabulary. Substitute "romance" for "cats" and you get a very good definition of the Tom in Sam Clemens. Tom's morality consisted of a fear of Aunt Polly's vindictive God until he came to distrust him, and an uncritical respect for the ethics of Hannibal. In spite of Susy, this was not entirely true of the adult Mark, and except in the Sawyer corner of his soul, it was not true of Sam Clemens either. For Tom indeed was too limited, too romantic, and too specialized in egoism, to hold all the inner life and outer experiences of Sam Clemens. He dominates the book that bears his name, in which Huck is little more than comic relief, yet it is significant that it is Huck at the end, not Tom, who speaks last in a passage of ideas, ideals, and realistic common sense of which Tom was incapable. Mark, in the epilogue to his story, promises, if it seems worthwhile, to describe in another book the boys after they become men. But when he came to write it, he found that there was much more left to say about the boy Huck, and made him the hero of what proved to be his greatest book.

For Huck proved to be quite as much Sam Clemens as was the show-off Tom, and the better and the deeper part. His dense ignorance of everything except the real essentials of life kept the fun going, but while cats, or at least dead ones, were his specialty, conscience and freedom were his two chief concerns. He hated the one and was a fanatic for the other. Shoes, stiff clothes, and school he knew how to escape from, but dad-rat it! he could never get away from a question of morals, which Tom slid round so easily. Huck, the son of a disreputable drunken failure, as Sam was the son of a frustrated lawyer, was a congenital product first of Westward-turning America, next of the backwoods, and most of all of the Mississippi. He was a tolerant cynic like the later Mark, suspicious of mankind, and he had the common sense which Tom lacked, and which Mark could use when he was not Tom. Huck was a river rat, a tough offspring of decadence like the London cockney, shrewd like a rat, kind like most vagabonds, a realist by necessity. . . .

AN INTIMATE TALE, WRITTEN WITH PASSION

I have tried . . . to identify one aspect at least of Sam Clemens' personality, temperament. and character with Tom Sawyer or Huck Finn. Now I shall try to separate them, as one must in discussing not a person but a book which projects, like all art, the author's imagination into the representative, the symbolical, and, if it is strong enough, into the universal. It is not a platitude to say that Tom is the eternal boy, but merely a too broad assertion that the success of *Tom Sawyer* is not to be explained only by the material Mark brought to the making of it.

There was nothing new in the nineteenth century at least in the subject—a small boy's biography. Before that century with its flood of humanitarianism, the child in neither Christian, nor Arabic, nor classic literature had seemed worthy of a book about him. Glimpses of children—pathetic, charming, ethical, or, as in the picaresque, immoral—are abundant. Shakespeare's Mamillius lives through a few speeches, Chaucer's Hugh of Lincoln in a few lines. But small boys and small girls in literature are usually seen but not heard, or are characters minor to the action. Their life, except that they should be kept alive, was neither interesting nor important to novelists of manners or pre-Wordsworthian poets, or philosophers before Rousseau. Yet after Thackeray and Dickens it would be absurd to call Twain the inventor of the boy's story. His originality must be sought elsewhere.

Mark wrote *Tom Sawyer* with passion, but he was curiously dubious of its merits and indifferent to its success except as a money-maker. In advance of reading, he offered Howells half the rights if he would dramatize it; and (incredible) when he did leave the manuscript with him to be read, said that if it got lost in the express on the way home, "it will be no great matter." Was there some reluctance at publishing so personal a story? We know that Livy was a good deal bothered in her respectable soul by some of the incidents, and more by items of language. Howells and she left one "hell" in by accident which came out in a hurry when Mark told Howells about it. Perhaps he had *Tom Sawyer* in mind when he told Orion that some day he would give up "bosh" written for others and please himself. Which, if you remember the real intimacy of the story, and its wide difference from his idea of a successful novel as illustrated by *The Gilded Age*, may account for some of his doubts. What is surprising, and very interesting, is that he wrote it for adults, meaning undoubtedly the innumerable perennial adolescents like himself, and it took Howells to persuade him that it should be edited and published as a boy's story for boys. For once Howells was wrong as an editor. The ideal audience for *Tom Sawyer* is the man recalling his youth. Boys read it for its excellent adventure, not always humorous; men, for a quality in Tom's imagination which they do not always understand.

THE PECULIAR QUALITY OF AN AMERICAN MASTERPIECE

The peculiar quality of *Tom Sawyer* is not easy to define. The graveyard murder, the trial, the Sunday School episode in which the tenderness of Mark's memory saved him for once from burlesque, the fabulous pirates' island, and more and more are easy to value—although I for one think that the cave and Becky and Injun Joe there and the hidden gold are on a very thin ice of contemporary sentimentalism. But none of these make it the so definitely *American* masterpiece that it unquestionably is. Part is in the realism of background, so vividly created that it may be said to have turned Mark Twain's small town on the river into a homing place for the American imagination. Compare in this respect another famous boy's book, Stevenson's *Treasure Island*, where pure adventure, if less humorous, is as memorable as in Mark's story. The literary merits of writing are said to be equal, though I do not agree. But Mark's hero is a projection of a personality infinitely deeper and more interesting than Stevenson's rather unoriginal youngster of pluck and invention lifted into adventure. Indeed, except for Long John Silver, *Treasure Island* would not be notable for personality. And the background of *Treasure Island* does not leave pictures that become part of the furnishing of memory, not even for tropical islands. For Stevenson at the time of writing had never seen a tropical island, and his scene is drawn from the coast range of Southern California, with even a redwood, California azalea, and improbable nutmeg trees from the East tossed in to make the island seem tropical.

Tom himself, I mean the Tom as Mark created him, not the Tom whose tricks and adventures were undoubtedly much like those of young Sam Clemens, was actually the Colonel Sellers [of Twain's *The Gilded Age*] of St. Petersburg. The analogy, like most analogies, is incomplete, but in essence it is true and convincing. The Obedstown where Colonel Sellers dreamed and ate raw turnips was by Mark's own merciless description a run-down backwoods settlement of the decadent survivors of the pioneers. The rail-sitting inhabitants were kindly and picturesque, yet that is all that could be said for them. They were, as the Colonel said, less industrious than their own pigs, no more forward-looking than their slaves—nomads camping in a land whose promise had only been scratched. It was the Colonel, his mind, like Don Quixote's, unsettled by too much reading, who gilded the doomed village until he believed all he said.

And what was St. Petersburg itself without the expansive imagination of Tom? A sluggish, lovable small town of the kind familiar to all Americans of the old stock, with only one half-breed Indian and stories of sordid river pirates to recall its less respectable past. Such it was in its own eyes, and it was only Tom's imagination that made it a memorable experience to have grown up there. For Tom was not only the eternal small boy who feared God and hated the Sunday School, but also the only begetter of romantic and heroic dreams drawn from what he could remember of his reading. The river was just a river to the tobacco-spitting loafers, but to Tom it became seas and deserts, and also to the boys he led, even to that eminent realist Huck Finn, until they got tired and went home. You can say of old Sellers and young Sellers, each in his way, what Chaucer said of Petrarch:

> *Petrak, who with rhetorike sweete,*
> *Enlumined all Ytaille with poesy.*

Only it was a very expansive, American type of rhetoric, with Southwestern trimmings.

THE STORY OF A NEW WORLD BOY

Most of all, *The Adventures of Tom Sawyer* is a story of a New World boy. Whatever its humor and its romance, the intoxicating element is freedom, freedom in this half-tamed river region of space, and freedom from effective control. Pap Finn complained bitterly of his loss of complete freedom which had led him like the Indians to take to drink. The boys, however, though still in the margin of regimented life, could be and were free to carry out anything Tom's inventive mind would propose. It was not only in their power, it was very definitely part of their share of the West-moving American tradition.

The Underlying Structure of *Tom Sawyer*

Robert Keith Miller

Robert Keith Miller notes that the episodic adventures of *Tom Sawyer* are bound by four story lines that share a common theme: death. Miller, who has written on Oscar Wilde as well as on Twain, finds other parallels among the story lines that bind the book into a cohesive whole.

To enter the world of *Tom Sawyer* is to step into a world in which barefoot boys go fishing on midsummer days, while prepubescent girls plan picnics on middle-class lawns and adults look beneficently on—dispensing ice cream, and advice that need not be taken seriously. The book offers to us a dream vision of American childhood. To be an American is to live on the edge of the frontier—but safely, behind a white picket fence in a town where everyone knows his neighbors and the sun beams down "like a benediction." And to be a child is to have adventures flavored with just enough anxiety to be genuinely exciting before returning, at will, to well-laden dinner tables and Sunday school socials. Rightly recognized as "the most amiable of all Mark Twain's novels,"[1] *The Adventures of Tom Sawyer* has been so thoroughly absorbed into the mainstream of American culture that "such incidents as the whitewashing of the fence are, like a familiar landscape, so intimate to our experience that their importance is easily forgotten."[2]

But a careful reading of *Tom Sawyer* reveals that childhood is not free of threats nor small towns free of fear. For all of its Norman Rockwell sort of charm, St. Petersburg,

1. Robert Regan, *Unpromising Heroes: Mark Twain and His Characters* (Berkeley: The University of California Press, 1966), p. 116 2. Bernard DeVoto, *Mark Twain's America* (Cambridge: The Riverside Press, 1932), p. 304

Missouri, is not as idyllic as it may seem at first glance. The Temperance Tavern serves liquor in a back room. The graveyard is in poor repair. And there are caves, nearby, in which one can easily be lost. Moreover, as Bernard DeVoto observed many years ago, the episodes at the core of the book "revolve around body-snatching, murder, robbery, and revenge."[3] In short, St. Petersburg may be the garden of American innocence, but it is a garden in which a serpent lurks.

FOUR STORY LINES

As the title of the book reminds us we are concerned here not so much with a carefully structured narrative as with a series of "adventures" that are bound together by virtue of the fact that they are the adventures of one particular boy. These adventures occasionally overlap, but they are, for the most part, independent of one another, making the action of the novel so episodic that an impatient critic may go so far as to declare "there is no plot."[4] There are, however, four loose story lines that help hold the work together.

The first of these stories begins when Tom witnesses the murder of Dr. Robinson. Tom had gone to the graveyard at midnight, together with his good friend Huckleberry Finn, in order to act out a ritual that is supposed to cure warts. Hiding behind a tombstone, they see that Robinson has engaged two grave robbers to supply him with a corpse, presumably for the study of anatomy. The boys recognize the robbers as Injun Joe, a half-breed, and Muff Potter, the town drunk. A quarrel breaks out over money, and Robinson knocks Potter unconscious just before he himself is stabbed by Injun Joe. The murderer thereupon puts the bloody knife into Potter's hand, convincing him—when he comes to—that he killed the doctor in a drunken fit.

The boys, of course, know otherwise, and when Potter is imprisoned for the murder, Tom undergoes a crisis of conscience. He is afraid to tell the truth, believing that Injun Joe might easily kill him too. But he cannot bear to see Potter executed for a crime he did not commit. Summoning all his courage, Tom eventually brings himself to testify at Potter's trial. His dramatic evidence secures the man's release, but Injun Joe escapes from town before he can be arrested.

3. Ibid., p. 306 4. George P. Elliott, "Vacation into Boyhood," afterword to *The Adventures of Tom Sawyer* (New York: New American Library, 1959), p. 221

Although Tom relishes the celebrity that comes to him as the star witness at a murder trial, "Injun Joe infested all his dreams," making his nights "seasons of horror." He finds distraction, however, in courting Becky Thatcher, the dimpled daughter of the local judge. The growing relationship between Tom and Becky provides the material for another "adventure." During an outing to the labyrinthine caves outside of town, Tom leads Becky away from their classmates, and exploring further than the others dare to go, they finally realize they are lost. They are trapped within the caves for three days, and desperate search parties are almost ready to give them up when Tom discovers an opening to the surface.

By this point in the novel, Tom has won Becky's heart. But earlier in the story, they quarrel after Becky learns that Tom had once been "engaged" to Amy Lawrence. Seeing himself as "forsaken," Tom decides to run away from home. Together with Huck Finn and Joe Harper, he heads for Jackson's Island in the middle of the Mississippi. The boys play at being pirates and have a glorious time roasting turtle eggs and learning how to smoke. But the townspeople come to believe that the boys must have drowned in the river, and in a scene that represents the fulfillment of many a child's fantasy, Tom sneaks ashore to watch his family mourn his death. He subsequently returns to the island, but only to wait for his own funeral, which he and his friends enjoy unseen before revealing themselves to the astonished congregation. The boys are welcomed back from the dead, and Tom and Becky are soon reconciled.

A fourth and final story concerns the fate of Injun Joe. He returns to town to take revenge not on Tom but on the Widow Douglas, whose husband had treated him harshly. He plans to "slit her nostrils" and "notch her ears like a sow"[5] but is overheard by Huck who runs for help, scaring the culprit away. Seeking refuge in the same caves that proved so dangerous to Tom and Becky, he is accidently trapped inside when Judge Thatcher has the entrance triple-locked with a "big door sheathed with boiler iron," in order to prevent anyone else from becoming lost within. Several weeks elapse before his plight becomes known. "When the cave door was unlocked, a sorrowful sight presented itself in

5. In the original manuscript, Injun Joe plans to rape the Widow Douglas. Twain was persuaded that this was unsuitable for a book that would be read by children. It seems odd, however, that slitting nostrils and notching ears was considered more acceptable.

the dim twilight of the place. Injun Joe lay stretched upon the ground, dead, with his face close to the crack of the door, as if his longing eyes had been fixed, to the latest moment, upon the light and the cheer of the free world outside."

The villain conveniently disposed of, the novel now draws to a close with Tom and Huck falling joint heir to a little over twelve thousand dollars in gold—buried treasure that had been unearthed by Injun Joe and hidden by him in the cave, where the boys find it. As a result of this discovery, Huck is drawn into the social organization of the town, his share of the fortune invested at six percent, and his welfare entrusted to the Widow Douglas, who promises to raise the boy who had saved her from injury. And great things are predicted for Tom. Judge Thatcher declares that he is "no commonplace boy" and in gratitude for leading Becky out of the cave, promises to send him to West Point and later to "the best law school in the country."

SEEMING INCONSISTENCIES

As the various threads of the narrative unfold, they sometimes seem at odds with one another. Tom comes from a home where apples are carefully rationed, but when he leaves for Jackson's Island he is able to steal a whole ham, the loss of which is never noticed. When Tom and Becky are in the cave, they are constantly coming across subterranean springs and even discover a large lake. But, in the conclusion of the Injun Joe story, Twain makes a great point of how the murderer died of thirst as well as starvation.[6] And . . . the characterization of Tom Sawyer is very uneven. His age is never specified, and it is difficult to picture him clearly. On Jackson's Island he acts like an eight-year-old, but in many of the scenes with Becky he seems closer to fourteen.

Twain also found it difficult to move from one story to another. When, for example, he wants to shift the scene from Jackson's Island back to St. Petersburg at the conclusion of chapter 16, he is forced to intrude rather awkwardly upon the text: "We will leave [the boys] to smoke and chatter and brag, since we have no further use for them at present." There is a large gap between chapter 24, which describes Tom's fear of Injun Joe, and chapter 25, which shows him

6. Henry Nash Smith makes this point in *Mark Twain: The Development of a Writer* (Cambridge: Harvard University Press, 1962), p. 84.

THE DEATH OF INJUN JOE

In this excerpt from his Autobiography, *Twain describes his reactions when he was a child on hearing of the death of the real Injun Joe—and his recovery from fear the following morning.*

I think that in *Tom Sawyer* I starved Injun Joe to death in the cave. But that may have been to meet the exigencies of romantic literature. I can't remember now whether the real Injun Joe died in the cave or out of it but I do remember that the news of his death reached me at a most unhappy time—that is to say, just at bedtime on a summer night, when a prodigious storm of thunder and lighting accompanied by a deluging rain that turned the streets and lanes into rivers caused me to repent and resolve to lead a better life. I can remember those awful thunder-bursts and the white glare of the lightning yet and the wild lashing of the rain against the windowpanes. By my teachings I perfectly well knew what all that wild rumpus was for—Satan had come to get Injun Joe. I had no shadow of doubt about it. It was the proper thing when a person like Injun Joe was required in the under world and I should have thought it strange and unaccountable if Satan had come for him in a less spectacular way. With every glare of lightning I shriveled and shrank together in mortal terror, and in the interval of black darkness that followed I poured out my lamentings over my lost condition, and my supplications for just one more chance, with an energy and feeling and sincerity quite foreign to my nature.

But in the morning I saw that it was a false alarm and concluded to resume business at the old stand and wait for another reminder.

The Autobiography of Mark Twain, edited by Charles Neider. New York: Harper, 1959.

cheerfully digging for treasure in a house he believes to be haunted. And Twain himself seems to realize that the conclusion to the novel is a bit abrupt, confessing, "When one writes a novel about grown people, he knows exactly where to stop—that is, with a marriage; but when he writes of juveniles, he must stop where he best can."

CREATING A COHESIVE WHOLE

Nevertheless, there are a number of parallels among the various plots that help bind the work into a cohesive whole. The most obvious of these is that each of the principal adventures concerns a death—either real or supposed. One story begins with the death of Dr. Robinson, and another ends with the death of Injun Joe. In the Jackson's Island episode, Tom pretends to be dead until he can enjoy a public triumph. And, in the cave sequence, Tom and Becky come very close to dying until—after three days—they rise from what might easily have been their tomb and return to town for the sort of joyful reunion that Tom has already experienced once before.

Moreover, the stories almost seem inevitable. They resolve themselves according to predictable patterns by drawing upon familiar myths, the most important of which are "the resurrection of the dead, the golden age, and the capture of the demon's hoard,"[7] as Robert Tracy has pointed out. Each of these myths is introduced as part of a game, but then realized by what actually comes to pass. The organization of the novel

> depends in large part on a kind of thematic resonance or echo: a myth, a superstition, or an incident from romance is evoked, and this is followed by a sudden startling realization of that myth or romance. The boys pretend to be pirates and find themselves tracked by a murderer. They speculate about treasure according to Tom's half-baked romantic ideas, and behold, a treasure appears. The haunted house *is* haunted, by dangerous criminals. They dream of a "Delectable Land" of freedom, and with the Jackson's Island episode they really do sojourn in that land. Tom imagines situations in which he will die for Becky, and then finds himself in a situation in which he must truly act heroically to save her life. . . . Reality is continually interpenetrated by the mythic and the romantic worlds.[8]

AN AMERICAN SUCCESS MYTH

But if much of *Tom Sawyer* has the familiarity of a fairy tale in which the hero ultimately wins the hand of a princess after a number of daring deeds, it also embodies another myth that is especially dear to the American heart. Among other things, it is a success story in which an orphan boy makes good, not through patience and industry, like Horatio Alger, but through imagination, self-reliance, and courage. Socially, Tom is not Becky's equal. He has only two sets of clothes, and there is an element of class antagonism in the enmity that immediately springs up between him and Alfred

7. Robert Tracy, "Myth and Reality in *The Adventures of Tom Sawyer,*" *The Southern Review*, 4 (Spring 1968), p. 534 8. Ibid., p. 536

Temple, "that St. Louis smarty that thinks he dresses so fine and is aristocracy." (It is significant that after Tom and Becky quarrel, the judge's daughter chooses Alfred Temple as her new beau. A sneak who pours ink on Tom's spelling book, he is, at least, a member of her own class.) Tom may be "a bad, vicious, vulgar child," but he's got pluck, a virtue that Americans never fail to admire. His adventures all have one thing in common—they testify to his need for recognition. As Robert Regan has observed,

> one element, motivation, unites all the actions. From first to last, young Thomas Sawyer, the orphan ward of a poor woman, a Sunday school scholar not noted for his studiousness, a frequent candidate for flogging in the regular school, and in every accepted sense a poor match for his younger brother, strives to win acceptance, admiration, love, and leadership, to win a place of some importance in his society.[9]

And as the book progresses, Tom is increasingly successful in achieving this goal. An early attempt to gain public recognition backfires when, after managing to pass himself off as the star pupil of his Sunday school class, he tells Judge Thatcher that the first two disciples were David and Goliath. But after this false step, he manages to do better. When he stages his own "death," his "fine joke" earns him temporary notoriety. When he testifies against Injun Joe in court, he becomes "a glittering hero once more—the pet of the old, the envy of the young." And when he not only leads Becky Thatcher out of the cave but unearths a fortune in gold, Tom fulfills his quest—he is "courted, admired, stared at" wherever he goes, and even his most casual remarks are "treasured and repeated." What child could ask for more?

It should thus be clear that episodic though it may be, *The Adventures of Tom Sawyer* is not without structure. While each of the adventures is a self-contained story, they ultimately come together to form a recognizable pattern. Not only do they parallel one another, they become increasingly serious, enabling the boy-hero to dominate those adults who were slow, at first, to recognize his true worth. Compared to *Life on the Mississippi*, there is relatively little extraneous material. And when we remember that *Tom Sawyer* anticipates that work by several years, we should recognize that its construction is relatively sophisticated.

9. Regan, pp. 116–17

Creating Well-Rounded Characters

Gladys Carmen Bellamy

Twain's inability to create realistic characters, especially when he made his heroes one-dimensionally
good, was his greatest weakness as an author, writes
Gladys Carmen Bellamy. Bellamy, who chose to focus on Twain's literary merit in her book, *Mark
Twain as a Literary Artist*, finds that he manages to
resolve that problem in *Tom Sawyer*. In this novel
Twain created a boy's world inhabited by characters
that intermix good and bad; in short, she finds, his
boy heroes are fully human.

In attempting an elucidation of what appears to be Mark
Twain's greatest weakness as a literary artist, there must be
considered the two extremes with which the true artist has
nothing to do: on one hand, there is a blithe, easy, blind optimism; on the other, a pessimism which amounts to the
chaos of despair. Both of these worlds escape into exaggeration. The great writer shuns both and selects for his medium
the broad middle-ground where the two fields overlap.
Viewing man as a social being, he recognizes the mixed nature of life, the blending of good and evil in mankind. F.O.
Matthiessen considers, with special reference to the writing
of tragedy, that the author must not only "have accepted the
co-existence of good and evil in man's nature, he must also
possess the power to envisage some reconciliation between
such opposites, and the control to hold an inexorable balance." And any literature, if it is to gain our assent to its significance and truth, must reflect the same acceptance and
the same control. Failing this balanced control, this artistic
tension between life forces, any conflicts the writer may picture must fail to give the illusion of human reality upon
which great art depends.

A BLACK-AND-WHITE WORLDVIEW

Mark Twain, the uncompromising idealist, was rarely able to bridge the gulf between the ideal and the actual by this inclusive acceptance of fact. . . . His friends usually appeared to him as robed in spotless white, while the great unknown mass of "the damned human race" he beheld, apparently, as garbed in hell's own black. It was only rarely that he was aware of people whose moral garments had a tinge of gray— that great majority who are such curious mixtures of heroism and cowardice, of gentleness and cruelty, of selfishness and generosity. The strongly lighted black-and-white extremes of his life view made him frequently incapable of attaining that "norm," the absence of which criticism has deplored in his work. He possessed, therefore, only at times a mental synthesis of life forces that could act as a frame of reference within which his characters might be allowed to struggle towards their human destinies—with many failings, yet somehow glorious.

When John Keats defined the tragic attitude as "the love of good and ill," he must have had in mind the sort of broad comprehension and courageous acceptance which [Nathaniel] Hawthorne later possessed. Mr. Matthiessen has referred to an "enchanted wholeness" in the mind of Hawthorne. In that mind, it seems, good and evil are both enclosed as within a magic circle; for Hawthorne, in his penetration of moral obliquity, seems sometimes to have an odd sort of affection for evil, simply because it is a part of every man. Mark Twain's knowledge of moral obliquity was a match for Hawthorne's; but there the likeness ends. For Mark Twain, whose experience of living, whose very sense of being alive, should have given him a sympathy far beyond that of Hawthorne (who felt himself lacking in these respects)—Mark Twain could enter that magic circle only at times. Often, he was disenchanted and thrust outside it; or he was working inside a circle partial and incomplete because he could not close the arc by an acceptance of the inevitable evil that accompanies the good of life. He therefore could not forge an artistic unity comparable to that of life itself—life as we know it.

The writer must reflect the world as he sees it. It can hardly be useful to him to demand that mankind be perfect; it will be more useful so to handle his materials that somehow beauty may be found. He need not have a beautiful world to deal with if he is able, as T.S. Eliot has said, "to see beneath both beauty and ugliness; to see the boredom, and the horror, and the glory." He must not flinch from the boredom and the horror; but he must manage somehow to make the glory apparent to his fellows, as bored and as horror-struck as he.

Mark Twain's is a mind in rebellion, a mind that flinches from what it sees and cannot accept it—cannot bear to look upon that chasm between the real and the ideal which opens before his horrified eyes. Consequently, his mind refuses to attempt the synthesis necessary for bringing the two aspects of life together within his consciousness, thus circumscribing and controlling his material and giving it what we think of as artistic form. This is, I believe, the reason that he could never write "a play that would play," in spite of what Howells called his "unequaled dramatic authority." For in a drama, beyond all other forms of literary art, there must be some sort of unity wrought out of diverse elements, a struggle in which is reached some solution forced as a momentary truce with life.

Textbooks, defining plot as that element which imparts form to the action, maintain that in a well-plotted play the events must be clearly related to each other in a chain of cause and effect; inevitability must arise from the sense that the character of the particular hero would allow of no other conclusion; and thus a structural entity, a feeling of completeness, is established. Among Mark Twain's most cherished ideas were his concepts of the inexorability of the cause-and-effect chain and the inevitability of every happening to every man. Yet he could never write "a play that would play." But there is another element necessary to drama: an appropriate conclusiveness derived from the sense of *alleviation* that must arise in the minds of the audience as the play moves to its end. The alleviation may come from a feeling that life has done its worst to the principals, leading to a sense of stoical calm; or it may arise from the sense that the characters' sufferings were brought about by weaknesses within themselves and thus their fate is preferable to the overthrow of the moral order which must ensue if they escape unpunished, undestroyed; or, as Mr. Matthiessen suggests, it may grow from recognition by the characters themselves of the justice of their fate, a recognition through which they participate "in the purgatorial movement, the movement towards regeneration." It is this sense of alleviation that Mark Twain, writing in bitterness, was frequently unable to inject into his material.

His moralism is itself an indication of his failure to see life whole. The moralizer tends to over simplify—to see life only in terms of black and white. He displays a partial, incomplete knowledge of man and reality through his overmastering urge to set the stage of life for those he would reform, furnishing it with certain selected props, arbitrarily excluding large areas of human activity and experience. . . .

THE GREATNESS OF THE BOY BOOKS

But in his books about boys—and this partly explains their greatness—he accepts the whole of life because he accepts the whole of boy nature, good and bad. In Hannibal he had seen both aspects of life. In Hannibal he had witnessed scenes of brutal violence, of absolute terror, of superstitious fear; and, because it remained for him both a summer idyll and a dark ground of horror, Hannibal was always the most fruitful setting for his work. The boy's world that he remembered had been full of charm; and yet his submerged consciousness recognized the dangers that had lurked beneath that surface of charm. Tom Sawyer's St. Petersburg, lying between the forest and the river, seems filled with a slow golden peace. It *seems* so. Jackson's Island was his Shangri La; but it was not a safe island, for life is not safe. Out of his steady apprehension of the terror of life, he wrote into the book that embodies his village idyll, as Mr. [Bernard] DeVoto has noticed, grave-robbing, revenge, murder, robbery, drowning, starvation, witchcraft and demonology, the malevolence of Injun Joe, and the fear of death that grips Tom and Becky lost in the cave and awaiting death in the dark. But after their emergence from the cave, the sun shines again and life goes on, much as before. And there is nowhere the suggestion that that life is not worth the living. Although inartistic in its minor effects—in the momentary impact of its melodramatic scenes, for instance—the book is ultimately satisfying because it has the artistic tension between life forces, the equilibrium necessary for art.

At Quarry Farm, in a small study shaped like a pilothouse, Mark Twain busied himself in the summer of 1874 with *Tom Sawyer.* Paine believed that he had begun the story in 1872 as a play; but perhaps this play was only an attempt to dramatize the story after it was written. In working among the Mark Twain Papers, DeVoto discovered some sheets labeled by Paine as "Boy's Manuscript," actually an early form of *Tom Sawyer.* Mr. DeVoto believes that this manuscript, in diary form, was written as early as 1870, which means that Tom Sawyer, rather than *The Gilded Age,* was Mark Twain's first attempt at fiction. In *Mark Twain at Work,* Mr. DeVoto has published the unfinished manuscript, and its relationship to Tom Sawyer is unmistakable, though the characters wear different names in the diary.

Mark Twain and Olivia Langdon were married on February 2, 1870. For months before and after that date his letters—to his mother, his sister, and his friends—were full of Livy, Livy, Livy. Setting the date of the "Boy's Manuscript" about 1870 suggests to me that the boy's diary may have been begun as a sort of playful, whimsical love letter to Olivia. The subject matter of the diary adds weight to this speculation.[1] But whatever the impulse that led him to set forth, when he was once started on that road of boyhood reminiscence the result was inevitable.

CRITICS DISAGREE

Constance Rourke wrote of Mark Twain that "he was never the conscious artist, always the improviser," and both Mr. DeVoto and Mr. [Edward] Wagenknecht have recorded their agreement. Recent study, however, has departed from this view—specifically, Walter Blair's analysis of *Tom Sawyer.* Mr. DeVoto holds, "Structurally, *Tom Sawyer* is a better job than most of Mark's fiction"; but he objects to "psychological anachronisms" in the boys and to the elastic time element

---

1. On the *Quaker City* excursion Mark Twain met Olivia's brother, Charley Langdon, fell in love with her picture in Charley's stateroom, and cultivated Charley's acquaintance thereafter. Billy Rogers wrote in his diary, "I've got acquainted with her brother Tom, and I expect he tells her about me. I'm always hanging around him." Boasting of Livy's charm to his mother, Mark Twain wrote: "Her father and mother and brother embrace and pet her constantly, precisely as if she were a *sweetheart.*" The diary reads: "How awful it is to meet her father and mother! They seem like kings and queens to me. And her brother Tom—I can hardly understand how it can be—but he can hug and kiss her whenever he wants to." Paine relates an amusing incident in which, as Mark Twain was leaving the Langdon home after a visit, an accident occurred and he fell out of a light wagon to the cobbled street. Mark Twain feigned injury and was carried into the house; Olivia was especially attentive, and his visit was prolonged two weeks. Billy Rogers confides to his diary: ". . . a man . . . nearly ran over me with his wagon. I wished he had, because then I would have been crippled and they would have carried me into her house all bloody and busted up, and she would have cried, and I would have . . . had to stay there till I got well, which I wish I never would get well." (*Mark Twain at Work,* 26.) All these passages occur in the first few pages of the manuscript.

which allows the Missouri summer to last far too long. Mr. Blair argues that if the book is viewed as Mark Twain's answer to the sentimental "Sunday school books" of the time, it takes on a new meaning which explains its structure; and even the time scheme may be defended as "a device contributing to developments important in the novel."

As the story opens, Tom is caught stealing jam, but he evades punishment by deceiving Aunt Polly. He plays hooky, attempts more deceit, and is exposed by Sid; he dashes out, threatening revenge. Later he meets a strange boy whom he hates at sight because of his neat clothes, licks the stranger, and then chases him home. By the end of the first chapter, Mr. Blair points out, in the hands of the moral writers Tom would stand committed as a Bad Boy. Tom continues on his unhallowed way, while Mark Twain chronicles him with gusto and even commends his chicanery in the whitewashing coup. Mark Twain summarizes Tom: "He was not the Model Boy of the village. He knew the model boy very well though—and loathed him."

Sid stands for the regulation Good Boy of the sentimentalized tales. Early in the book Mark Twain describes Huck Finn, the "juvenile pariah of the village," the envy of all the other boys because of his "gaudy outcast condition," who doubtless would appear in the moralized literature as a sort of Super Bad Boy:

> Huckleberry came and went, at his own free will. . . . he did not have to go to school or to church . . .; he could go fishing or swimming when and where he chose. . . . he never had to wash, nor put on clean clothes; he could swear wonderfully. In a word, everything that goes to make life precious, that boy had. So thought every harassed, hampered, respectable boy in St. Petersburg.

Mr. Blair suggests that Mark Twain held the additional motive of showing his readers that boyish pranks are a natural means of development. Although he saw the adult world in a different light, he could grant that a real boy was not simply good or bad, but a mixture of virtue and mischief. "If *Tom Sawyer* is regarded as a working out . . . of this notion of a boy's maturing," says Mr. Blair, "the book will reveal . . . a structure . . . quite well adapted to its purpose." Under a patterning of action which shows a boy developing, Mr. Blair finds four units of narrative: the story of Tom and Becky; the Jackson's Island episode; the story of Tom and

Muff Potter; and the Injun Joe story. In the boy-and-girl story, Tom begins with a fickle desertion of Amy and winds up by taking Becky's punishment at school and later manfully guarding her in the cave. The Jackson's Island episode begins with Tom's childish revolt against Aunt Polly, which spurs him to run away, and ends with his concern for his aunt's uneasiness about him. The Muff Potter story begins with the superstitious trip of Tom and Huck to the graveyard and ends with Tom's defiance of superstition in testifying for Muff Potter. In the Injun Joe story, which begins with a boyish search for buried treasure, the development is concerned more with Huck than with Tom: Huck conquers his fear of Injun Joe to rescue the Widow Douglas from the dangerous renegade. Of the thirty-five chapters, only four are not in some way concerned with one of these narrative units, and of these four, one is the first and necessarily expository chapter.

Considered thus, the structural pattern refutes Mr. [Carl] Van Doren's objection that the book is "overloaded with matters brought in . . . when no necessity calls for them," as well as Mr. DeVoto's objection that Tom has "no nebulous, inarticulate vision of growing up," no notion of "the strengths, the perceptions, and the failures that will eventually make a man." Having traced Tom through a number of situations in which his actions grow less and less irresponsible and more and more mature, Mr. Blair directs attention to Mark Twain's conclusion of the book as an indication that he himself was fully aware of this structural pattern: "So endeth this chronicle. It being strictly the history of a *boy*, it must stop here; the story could not go much further without becoming the history of a *man*."

WELL-ROUNDED LIFE IN THE VILLAGE

When the Welshman said that Huck had "good spots" in him, the Widow Douglas agreed: "That's the Lord's mark. He don't leave it off. . . . Puts it somewhere on every creature that comes from his hands." That Mark Twain viewed the life of his village as rounded and whole is revealed in such passages. Mr. DeVoto explains the hold Hannibal had over his imagination on the ground that "when he invoked Hannibal he found there not only the idyll of boyhood but anxiety violence, supernatural horror, and an uncrystallized but enveloping dread." Perhaps this means simply that Mark Twain had recognized in Hannibal the twofold aspect of life.

His view of Hannibal as twofold explains the artistry he achieves in his fiction grounded there. Bringing the boy-world into a proper focus, he gains the same sort of perspective he attains in viewing the world of the blacks. The wholeness of these two worlds is attested by his recognition that boys can lie and that slaves can feel sexual desire; that developing boys can be mixtures of good and bad, and that the blacks—as embodied in Roxy [in *Pudd'nhead Wilson*]— can be malicious and vengeful, loyal and loving, thieving and tipsy, self-sacrificing and courageous. Through this perspective, he is enabled to discern the forces of good and evil held in the tension that art demands. The result is that even the pettiness of the village Sunday school in *Tom Sawyer* is handled with a detachment which robs it of his customary scorn. The book has the permanency of a beautiful fairy tale. The golden haze of Tom Sawyer's summer enshrouds it; and Mark Twain was right when he said of it, "*Tom Sawyer* is simply a hymn, put into prose to give it a worldly air."

Shaping the Manuscript

Bernard DeVoto

Bernard DeVoto succeeded Albert Bigelow Paine as the literary executor of the Twain estate, a position eminently suited for his study of Twain's working habits and editorial practices. The relatively few changes Twain made in *Tom Sawyer* show the influence of his friend William Dean Howells, editor of *Atlantic Monthly*, and of his wife, Livy, DeVoto reports. Some of the revisions made to "clean up" the language removed phrasings DeVoto regrets losing, but others improved the story line and Twain's style.

Mark began writing [*Tom Sawyer*] as we now know it in either 1873 or 1874 (on the whole, the latter seems the likelier year), and on July 5, 1875, told [William Dean] Howells that he had finished it. His episodic method of composition shows in the book's handsome indifference to minutiae. Judge Thatcher [appeared] as Judge Fletcher in a middle section. . . . This was rectified in the manuscript but a confusion in the relationships and residence of the Thatcher family survives in the book. The Judge ends by swallowing Lawyer Thatcher, whom he is visiting when he first appears, and by the end of the book is a permanent resident of St. Petersburg, though half-way through it his home is still Constantinople, which had originally been called Coonville in the manuscript. (He is still in St. Petersburg in *Huckleberry Finn*, but his daughter Becky has become Bessie.) Mr. Dobbins's school is larger at the ceremonies of graduation than when we first see the classes reciting. Tom's enchanted summer is similarly elastic: the season is not yet over when the Widow Douglas gives her party for the boys, but if you count the weeks that have elapsed since the Fourth of July you will find that autumn should be well along. There are other incongruities, inconsistencies, and loose ends. They do not matter at all but they are the sort of thing that Arnold

Bennett had in mind when he called Mark Twain "the divine amateur." Bennett was a type-specimen of the professional writer, whose pride of craft it is to leave nothing undigested, to tie all knots and sandpaper all joints till the parts are perfectly fitted in a whole. Mark Twain was at times superior to and always incapable of such discipline. He had the discipline of daily work and the sterner discipline that made his prose one of the great styles of English, but he lacked the discipline of revision and the discipline that makes a writer uneasy until his material has been completely thought through into form. That lack is his greatest defect as an artist; it is rather less evident in *Tom Sawyer* than in most of his novels but sometimes it shows clearly.

EDITING SUGGESTIONS FROM HOWELLS

Finishing his book, Mark was eager to submit it to his arbiter and censor, Howells.[1] The letter of July 5, 1875, asks Howells to read it "and point out the most glaring defects"— and Mark is then of the opinion that "It is *not* a boy's book, at all. It will only be read by adults. It is only written for adults." Howells's summer plans deferred his reading and there was no hurry, for both the English and American publishers were awaiting a more favorable time for publication. An amanuensis [secretary's] copy of the manuscript (now privately owned) was prepared, and this is the one which Howells read the following November and on which he made his annotations. On November 21, he wrote to Mark:

> I finished reading *Tom Sawyer* a week ago, sitting up till one A.M. to get to the end, simply because it was impossible to leave off. It's altogether the best boy's story I ever read. It will be an immense success. But I think you ought to treat it explicitly *as* a boy's story. Grown-ups will enjoy it just as much if you do; and if you should put it forth as a study of boy character from the grown-up point of view, you'd give the wrong key to it. I have made some corrections and suggestions in faltering pencil, which you'll have to look for. They're almost all in the first third. When you fairly swing off, you had better be left alone. The adventures are enchanting. I wish *I* had been on that island. The treasure-hunting, the loss in the cave, it's all exciting and splendid. I shouldn't think of pub-

1. He had apparently discussed the book with Howells while he was working on the last part of it. In an unpublished letter of June 21, 1875, he wrote: "Thank you ever so much for the praises you give the story. I am going to take into consideration all you have said, and then make up my mind by and by. Since there is no plot to the thing, it is likely to follow its own drift, and so is as likely to drift into manhood as anywhere—I won't interpose. If I only had the Mississippi book written, I would surely venture this story in the Atlantic." Note this further revelation of his aimlessness.

lishing this story serially. Give me a hint when it's to be out, and I'll start the sheep to jumping in the right places.

I don't seem to think I like the last chapter. I believe I would cut that.[2]

Mark wrote at once (November 23) "As to that last chapter, I think of just leaving it off and adding nothing in its place. Something told me that the book was done when I got to that point—and so the strong temptation to put Huck's life at the Widow's into detail, instead of generalizing it in a paragraph was resisted." The meaning of this is cloudy but the present stilted "Conclusion" has been added to the amanuensis copy in Mark's own hand, and that may indicate that there was another chapter—that *Adventures of Huckleberry Finn* began prematurely in *Tom Sawyer.*

Illness kept Mark from making revisions until January, when, on the 18th, he wrote to Howells:

There was never a man in the world so grateful to another as I was to you day before yesterday, when I sat down (in still rather wretched health) to set myself to the dreary and hateful task of making final revision of Tom Sawyer, and discovered, upon opening the package of MS that your pencil marks were scattered all along. This was splendid, and swept away all labor. Instead of *reading* the MS, I simply hunted out the pencil marks and made the emendations which they suggested. I reduced the boy battle to a curt paragraph; I finally concluded to cut the Sunday school speech down to the first two sentences, leaving no suggestion of satire, since the book is to be for boys and girls [his opinion has changed since July]; I tamed the various obscenities until I judged that they no longer carried offense. So, at a single sitting I began and finished a revision which I supposed would occupy 3 or 4 days and leave me mentally and physically fagged out at the end. [Mark's conception of revision shows in this estimate.]

Most of Howells's suggestions can still be made out in the margins of the amanuensis copy. Mark seems to have adopted all of them, but there are fewer than the letters suggest. At the end of Chapter III, Howells writes, "Don't like this chapter much. The sham fight is too long. Tom is either too old for that or too young for [word or words lost]. Don't like the chaps in [word or words lost]." Obediently Mark cuts some three hundred words from the sham battle, much to its improvement. (He missed one word, however, which remained a meaningless vestige in all editions of the book till 1939. Tom rode a broomstick horse in that battle, and later he made it "cavort" in front of Becky's house. At his final departure the text has hitherto inexplicably read, "Finally he rode home reluctantly with his poor head full of visions.") Mr. Walters's speech in Sunday school has been improved by its reduction. A speech of Joe Harper's before the venture in piracy has been cleared of burlesque. Howells objects to "cussedness" as a Yankee expression and Mark makes it "Old Scratch." Howells checks Alfred Temple's "Aw—what a long tail our cat's got" (which Mark had already substituted for "Aw—go blow your nose") and it comes out "Aw—take a walk." Where Tom now says, in the next speech, that he will "bounce a rock off'n your head," Howells has objected, soundly, to "mash your mouth." There are perhaps a half-dozen further stylistic changes, as where Tom's "throes of bliss" on receiving the Barlow knife become a "convulsion of delight," and where his original intention to "gloom the air with a lurid lie" is altered to "take refuge in a lie." But more interesting and important are the mild "obscenities" that Mark mentions in his letter.

"CLEANING UP" THE MANUSCRIPT

Howells cannot be charged with the change of "the devil" to "Satan" toward the end of the book nor (I think—the copy is not clear) with the softening of "foul slop" to "water" where the Thatcher's maid drenched the adoring Tom, whose "reeking" garments are then made merely "drenched." Mark had also softened Injun Joe's intentions toward the Widow Douglas. His original explanation that to get revenge on a woman "you cut her nose off—and her ears" had been altered to "you slit her nostrils—you notch her ears" when the amanuensis copy was made, and where Huck now tells the Welshman that he heard "the Spaniard swear he'd spile her looks" he originally added "and cut her ears off." Perhaps Olivia Clemens or Mark's children had shrunk from these expressions, though more likely it was Mark's own nerves that flinched. But Howells's nerves required further alterations.

The poodle which relieves the suffering of the congregation by sitting down on a pinchbug now goes "sailing up the aisle" and no more; but originally he sailed up that aisle "with his tail shut down like a hasp." Howells writes in the margin, "Awfully good but a little too dirty," and an amusing phrase goes out. Much more important, by far the most important change anywhere in the manuscript is the modification of Chapter XX. Here, in the margin opposite Becky Thatcher's stolen glimpse of "a human figure, stark naked" in Mr. Dobbins's textbook of anatomy, Howells writes, "I should be afraid of this picture incident," and so cancels one of the truest moments of childhood in the manuscript. Reproached by Becky for sneaking up on her, Tom had originally said, "How could *I* know it wasn't a nice book? I didn't know girls ever—." Becky's apprehension of being whipped carried a postscript, "But that isn't anything—it ain't *half.* You'll tell everybody about the picture, and O, O, *O!*" Meditating on what a curious kind of fool a girl is, Tom was originally permitted to think:

> But that picture—is—well, now it ain't so curious she feels bad about that. No. . . [Mark's punctuation] No, I reckon it ain't. Suppose she was Mary and Alf Temple had caught her looking at such a picture as that and went around telling. She'd feel— well, I'd lick him. I bet I would. [Then, farther toward the end of the soliloquy] Then Dobbins will tell his wife about the picture. [Note the information that Dobbins is married.]

And Becky was originally permitted to think, "He'll tell the scholars about that hateful picture—maybe he's told some of them before now."

The omission of this, the single allusion to sex in the book (which, observe, had survived the scrutiny of Olivia Clemens), is very interesting. The omission is clearly chargeable to Howells, and yet I suspect that Mark himself would soon have felt uneasy and, in manuscript or in proof, would have deleted those sentences on his own initiative. We are told that his anecdotes and conversation could be plentifully obscene and there is the published *1601* as well as the unpublished speech to the Stomach Club, "Some Thoughts on the Science of Onanism," and several other fragments, as well as some savage satires written during his last years but not intended to be published. Nevertheless he was almost lustfully hypersensitive to sex in print; he was in fact, as a writer, rather more prudish than Howells. His timorous circumlocutions, published and unpublished, are astonishing; he once argued that there could be no such thing as an age of consent, for all seduction was essentially rape; and, in an unpublished venture of Tom and Huck into the Indian country, he was as tremulous as a Bertha M. Clay when he had to suggest what might happen to a captured heroine. Of thirty-nine notebooks kept as banks of deposit for his books, only three contain any entries at all that deal with sex, and one of these does not contemplate its use for fiction. In *The Gilded Age* even a false marriage (whose daring presence in the book, besides, is probably due to Charles Dudley Warner) must be atoned for with a heroine's death—and, in short, of all Mark's published fiction only *Pudd'nhead Wilson* is aware of sexual desire as a human motive. Certainly childhood as he depicts it is naturally sexless—and he would probably have removed this blemish without Howells's warning.

EDEN BEFORE THE FALL

Mark could not have written about boyhood as it appears in the works of Sigmund Freud even if he had thought of it in that way, but there is no evidence that he thought of it as otherwise than sexless. Boyhood existed forever in the idyll of Hannibal, and he remembered Hannibal as he was to make Eve remember Eden, as an eternal summer before the Fall. The published *Autobiography* makes this clear, and the Mark Twain Papers contain many unpublished manuscripts and groups of notes that embody his memories of Hannibal. One of these manuscripts, "Villagers of 1840–43," is specially pertinent here. In the course of discussing many of Mark's neighbors it notes that some of the Blankenship girls (they would be Huck Finn's sisters) were charged with prostitution but adds, "not proven." It chronicles one adultery, one crime of passion, and one free union. Then it summarizes the subject in a separate paragraph:

> *Chastity.* There was the utmost liberty among young people—but no young girl was ever insulted, or seduced, or even scandalously gossiped about. Such things were not even dreamed of in that society, much less spoken of and referred to as possibilities.

Ever, not even dreamed of, possibilities! Those are emphatic words but Mark meant them. Whatever the defect of experience or recognition that made him thus libel a full-blooded folk, that is how he remembered Eden.

"IT WON'T DO FOR THE CHILDREN"

Before this essay no one, I think, had noticed the softening of Chapter XX, but Howells's remaining modification has become famous. Curiously enough, he missed the offense when he read the manuscript. He did encounter in Huck's passionate grievance against the Widow Douglas, "she'd gag when I spit," and that had to go, but he passed "they comb me all to hell" without questioning it. But Mark had already spent some concern on the phrase—writing "hell," then changing it to "thunder," and finally restoring the dreadful word—and demanded judgment from his arbiter. In the letter of January 18, 1876, already quoted he said:

> There was one expression which perhaps you overlooked. When Huck is complaining to Tom of the rigorous system in vogue at the widow's, he says the servants harass him with all manner of compulsory decencies, and he winds up by saying: "and they comb me all to hell." (No exclamation point.) Long ago, when I read that to Mrs. Clemens, she made no comment;[5] another time I created occasion to read that chapter to her aunt and her mother (both sensitive and loyal subjects of the kingdom of heaven, so to speak) and *they* let it pass. I was glad, for it was the most natural remark in the world for that boy to make (and he had been allowed few privileges of speech in the book); when I saw that you, too, had let it go without protest, I was glad, and afraid, too—afraid you hadn't observed it. Did you? And did you question the propriety of it? Since the book is now professedly and confessedly a boy's and girl's book, that darn word bothers me some, nights, but it never did until I had ceased to regard the volume as being for adults.

Howells wrote, the next day:

> As to the point in your book: I'd have that swearing out in an instant. I suppose I didn't notice it because the locution was so familiar to my Western sense, and so exactly the thing that Huck would say. But it won't do for the children.[4]

So the expletive joined the simile about the poodle's tail and Tom's meditations about a naked figure in a textbook.

Mark's own changes in the manuscript are usually stylistic and always for the best. It is interesting to discover that Injun Joe's companion in the grave-robbing was originally Old Man Finn. He became Muff Potter, no doubt, to prevent Huck's oath from putting his father's life in jeopardy. And there is one deletion which not only suggests that there was

3. In his *Biography* (p. 549) [Albert Bigelow] Paine quotes from a letter which he does not print in the *Letters*: "Mrs. Clemens received the mail this morning, and the next minute she lit into the study with danger in her eye and this demand on her tongue: where is the profanity Mr. Howells speaks of? Then I had to miserably confess that I had left it out when reading the MSS. to her. Nothing but almost inspired lying got me out of this scrape with my scalp. Does your wife give you rats, like this, when you go a little one-sided?" This would seem to contradict the statement of January 18, 1876. Actually, however, Paine had misdated the letter and misunderstood the allusion. The profanity to which Livy was objecting was not "She combs me all to hell," was not even in *Tom Sawyer*—it was in "Old Times on the Mississippi." 4. Letter of January 19, 1876, in the Mark Twain Papers; never printed in full.

another intermediate stage of the book but also makes one thankful that, though Mark was tempted, he found grace to resist the kind of extravaganza that defaces the last quarter of *Huckleberry Finn.* At the end of Chapter III, Tom, saddened by Aunt Polly's cruelty, goes down to the river, where he sits on a raft in the darkness, takes out his wilted flower, and thinks of Becky with the melancholy that made Burton diagnose love as a neurosis. And "at last," the text says, "he rose up sighing and departed in the darkness." Until Mark crossed out the passage, the manuscript went on, "A dimly defined, stalwart figure emerged from behind a bundle of shingles upon the raft, muttering 'There's something desperate breeding here,' and then dropped stealthily into the boy's wake." There is no telling what wild notion was in Mark's mind but he was beginning to burlesque a passage already strained to the breaking-point and, remembering such passages elsewhere that he did not strike out, one is overjoyed to see heavy ink cancelling this one in time.

CHAPTER 2

The Individual and the Community in Tom Sawyer's World

READINGS ON
THE ADVENTURES
OF TOM SAWYER

Tom Sawyer: Performer and Chief Entertainer

James M. Cox

By indulging and applauding Tom's romantic "heroics," the people of St. Petersburg support the idea of the world as both playground and a play, writes James M. Cox. Since play is the reality of the book, Cox finds, Tom's ability to enjoy a spontaneous make-believe world makes him seem more real than the dull adults around him. Besides his book on Twain, Cox has also written on Robert Frost.

There are four essential elements which make up the world of Tom Sawyer. First there is, of course, the figure of Tom himself, standing at the center of the stage. Second, there is the stage, the summer world of St. Petersburg. Third, there is the audience—the society of St. Petersburg, composed of adults as well as children, all of whom function at one time or another as Tom's audience inside the action. Finally, there is the narrator, who acts as an indulgent audience himself. Though he exercises as much power over his characters as Thackeray does in *Vanity Fair*, the narrator creates the illusion of being a spectator who draws the curtain at his performance rather than a puppet master pulling the strings. Although the perspective upon the characters is equally remote in both novels, Thackeray exercises control in terms of plot and history, Mark Twain in terms of age and time. Thackeray's genius, following mock-heroic strategies, reduces adult rituals and momentous events to the status of acts upon a dwarfed stage. Tom Sawyer and his gang, on the other hand, are children at play—their world is a play world in which adult rituals of love, death, war, and justice are reenacted in essentially harmless patterns. To be sure there is violence in the play world of Tom Sawyer, and Bernard DeVoto was in a certain way right to observe that the idyl of

Hannibal is surrounded by dread. Yet the boy's world is charmed; it is safe simply because the narrator's perspective enchants whatever terror and violence exist inside the world. Like the "once upon a time" of the fairy tale, this perspective reduces the size of the action by keeping it at a distance from the reader.

The distance is maintained in two ways—through the perspective of burlesque and the perspective of indulgence. Franklin Rogers, in his study of Mark Twain's burlesque patterns, observes that . . . the first part of *Tom Sawyer* burlesques the good-boy cliché by showing how a bad boy prospers.[1] The soundness of Rogers' observations is evident throughout *Tom Sawyer*, from the blustering fight in the first chapter to the discovery of the treasure in the last. The relationship between Tom and Becky burlesques romantic conventions; the conversions of Tom and Huck, after the graveyard murder, parody religious conversions; lamentations of the village over Tom's apparent death mock funeral rituals and conventional language of grief. In brief, the entire action of the boys' world burlesques adult rituals.

And yet *Tom Sawyer* is neither burlesque nor primarily satiric novel. The reason is that the narrator's impulse toward burlesque and satire is largely assimilated in his indulgent posture. The burlesque personality of Mark Twain has undergone a genuine transformation. No longer the traveler or autobiographer, he is the observer of an action which, though intimate, is so remote in time that he patronizes the behavior of the actors at almost every point. The second chapter begins:

> Saturday morning was come, and all the summer world was bright and fresh, and brimming with life. . . .

Thus the scene is set, the idyl defined. In this scene the whitewashing episode takes place. The opening sentence of Chapter IV, "The sun rose upon a tranquil world, and beamed down upon the peaceful village like a benediction," provides an unobtrusive but nevertheless clearly evident "screen" for the Sunday school recitations. In Chapter XIV, Tom awakens on Jackson's Island. . . . Each of these passages at once qualifies and generalizes the scene—qualifies it by screening out the impact of unpleasurable impulses; generalizes it by stabilizing and stylizing action into the

1. Rogers, *Burlesque Patterns*, pp. 102–104

form of tableau. Though there is murder in the world, its impact does not reach the reader but is used up in the explosion it has upon the boys who move at a great distance from the reader. And though there is "realism" in the book, if one means by realism an antitype of romance, there is neither uniqueness of character nor particularity of incident. Instead of individuals, the book generates types. Thus there is not even a minute description of Tom Sawyer; it is impossible to tell what he looks like—how tall, how heavy, how handsome or ugly he is. He emerges as the figure, the *character* of the Boy. Yet he is not allegorical, simply because he is a *character* and not a personification.[2]. . .

A Performer with Two Audiences

The fact that the society of St. Petersburg, both old and young, is involved in watching Tom's play from the inside world of the novel while the narrator is engaged in watching it indulgently from the outside goes far toward creating Tom's role of chief actor in a drama which the juvenile reader can believe and the adult reader can indulge with a mixture of nostalgia and gentle irony. The narrator, an almost invisible agent with whom the adult reader unwittingly identifies, provides the perspective through which Mark Twain meant to reach an adult audience.[3] What Mark Twain did was to treat his fiction as a performance rather than a story. If, in the preface, he alluded to the adult audience he was creating, he defined the nature of his characters in the conclusion. "Most of the characters that perform in this book still live," he said, "and are prosperous and happy." He continued, "Some day it may seem worth while to take up the story of the younger ones again and see what sort of men

2. Mark Twain's characterization of Tom Sawyer is similar in method to Chaucer's in the *Canterbury Tales.* Two assumptions lie at the base of such characterization: (1) that people are not unique but ultimately similar in motive and behavior; (2) that social and psychological reality are wedded rather than divorced. Thus neither Chaucer nor Mark Twain develops characters with singular personalities; rather, they emphasize the traits, motives, and behavior which are easily recognizable by being individually manifest yet socially held in common. Thus, also, they have the capacity to typify characters (as knight, miller, friar, or boy) without in any way seeming to threaten their individuality. Indeed, both Chaucer and Mark Twain achieve the effect of reinforcing individuality by emphasizing typifying aspects of character. 3. After initially recommending that Mark Twain take Tom Sawyer on into manhood, [William Dean] Howells, upon seeing the manuscript, wrote: "It will be an immense success. But I think you ought to treat it explicitly *as* a boy's story. Grown-ups will enjoy it just as much if you do; and if you should put it forth as a study of a boy character from the grown-up point of view, you'd give the wrong key to it" (*Mark Twain–Howells Letters,* I, 110–11). In seeing it as a boy's story, Howells [editor of *Atlantic Monthly*] was evidently advising Mark Twain to avoid the narrow *Atlantic* audience in favor of the mass audience, advice Mark Twain was eager enough to have.

and women they turned out to be; therefore it will be wisest not to reveal any part of their lives at present." Here in the midst of the conventional Victorian epilogue is the disclosure that Mark Twain visualizes his characters in performance rather than in action, on stage rather than in the world.

Though the sense of a double audience contributes greatly to the illusion of a performance, there is still the performer—the actor and his "act." Tom Sawyer fully collaborates with the audience watching him; he puts on a show throughout the novel, one of the chief aspects of his character being his desire to be stage center. He is a performer in almost everything he does, whether he is showing off for Becky, parading with Joe and Huck into the arena of his own funeral, becoming the central figure in the trial of Muff Potter, or proudly producing the bags of gold before the startled eyes of St. Petersburgers. In a word, he is the show-off, and though he is not simply that, he cannot resist the temptation to perform to an audience. Thirty years after the writing of *Tom Sawyer*, Mark Twain observed that Theodore Roosevelt was a political incarnation of Tom Sawyer. "Just like Tom Sawyer," he remarked of Roosevelt's eagerness to keep the public eye; "always showing off."[4] This sense of showmanship defines Tom's desire to be a hero, for it is the spectacle of heroism as much as its achievement which fascinates Tom. The narrator gives us the image: "Tom was a glittering hero once more," he observes after Tom's performance at the trial, and the adjective tells the story. Tom simply has to shine if he can, and he utilizes every resource at his command to do so. . . .

HEROIC ACHIEVEMENT IN AN ENCHANTED WORLD

But Tom is a boy. His age, his size, and the security of his world—accentuated by the adult perspective upon it—place severe limits on the range of effects he can achieve. There are two areas of heroic achievement open to him in this enchanted world. The one is to be a hero on the St. Petersburg stage—in Becky's eye, the school's, the church's, the court's, or the town's. The other is to be victorious in the world of make-believe, in the world of play. Tom's genius lies in his ability to realize the possibilities of make-believe in the life

4. *Mark Twain in Eruption*, ed. Bernard DeVoto (New York, 1940), p. 49

of the village, combining both possibilities of achievement into a single act. Thus he succeeds in playing out his fantasies for the entertainment and salvation of the town.

The best example is the mock funeral, the motive or seed of which appears in the long passage in which Tom wants to die temporarily. At this early moment of the book, it is no more than a desire, an almost ineffectual and childish death wish which the narrator can patronize. But in the course of the narrative not only does Tom's wish become a reality—if that were all, the book would be no more than a juvenile success story—but the entire village is made to play the dupe in the performance. And not simply made to play the dupe but made to like the role.

The boy's resurrection, occurring precisely at the center of the book, is the central episode. By central, I mean characteristic or characterizing, for it dramatizes the full union between narration and action. First, the narrator sets the scene. In contrast to the joyous plans of the fugitives on Jackson's Island, he describes the village grief:

> But there was no hilarity in the little town that same tranquil Saturday afternoon. The Harpers, and Aunt Polly's family, were being put into mourning, with great grief and many tears. An unusual quiet possessed the village, although it was ordinarily quiet enough, in all conscience. The villagers conducted their concerns with an absent air, and talked little; but they sighed often. The Saturday holiday seemed a burden to the children. They had no heart in their sports, and gradually gave them up.

The two adjectives in the initial sentence define the narrator's visual and auditory perspective on the action. He discloses to the reader a scene so remote in distance that the village is a *little* town hung in a tranquil air. This distance is not something physical or definite in time and space—the narrator never says that the action happened so many miles away or so many years ago—but an objectification of a mental state. Thus the action and scene which the narrator unfolds in his first paragraph do not have the status of actuality; they are themselves an image, an idyl, which reflects in turn the narrator's role of complacent and superior observer.

His superiority is not simply one of size and actuality; it is superiority of knowledge which he shares with the reader. For the villagers do not know what the narrator and his readers are only too aware of—that Tom is not dead. Thus their grief, though real to them, is ultimately unreal because it has a false object and the narrator is free to ridicule it at will. He accomplishes his burlesque by exposing the clichés of conventional grief. The entire episode is handled remarkably, for the target of the burlesque—the threadbare clichés of conventional grief—is perfectly paralleled by the nature of the villagers' grief, which like their platitudes, is *sincere*, but nevertheless essentially unreal.

Tom's resurrection before the stunned townspeople who have ceremoniously gathered to lament his death is the surprise performance which he has prepared for the purpose of electrifying his audience. For Tom it is the act by which he gains the center of the stage; he has carefully made the resurrection his drama in which Huck and Joe will be supporting actors. Tom, completely unaware of the burlesque, remains imprisoned in his ego. While the choir bursts into song, "Tom Sawyer the Pirate looked around upon the envying juveniles about him and confessed in his heart that this was the proudest moment of his life."

AN INDULGENT COMMUNITY

In the world of *Pudd'nhead Wilson*, such a practical joke would have provided the source of unrelenting hostility and hatred, but here in the idyl, where burlesque commingles with indulgence, the townspeople are tolerant of Tom's boyish pranks and forgive him, as does his Aunt Polly, for making them ridiculous. They expect him to be bad and, like Aunt Polly, they love him for it—not because Mark Twain's world is "realistic" but because they are his audience and collaborate with Tom in creating the illusion that the world is ultimately given over to play. Thus what was to have been a funeral is transmogrified by Tom into an entertainment, enhancing rather than undermining the burlesque element. For Tom's joke, his play funeral, provides the ultimate definition of what the "sincere" funeral was to have been for the town in the first place—an entertainment! A tearful, lugubrious, and hackneyed production in which each of the participants was fully working up his part—but an entertainment nonetheless.

Tom's resurrection offers in fairly clear outline the essential realization of his character. He is of course the bad boy, but not simply the bad boy, though he breaks rules and plays practical jokes. Thomas Bailey Aldrich's Tom Bailey in *The Story of a Bad Boy* broke rules, and Peck's Bad Boy existed

by means of an endless succession of practical jokes on his
Pa. Neither is it Tom's subtler psychology nor his more realistic character which set him apart. Nor is it his celebrated
independence and pluck, nor his essentially good heart.
Tom is really no freer than Sid and clearly has no better
heart. Though the indulgent Mark Twain felt a deep invita-
tion to sentimentalize Tom in this way and thus affirm that
he was for all his badness really a good good boy, the burlesque perspective afforded protection against such sentimentality. As it had been for Mark Twain in the beginning
and as it was throughout his career, burlesque functioned as
a reality principle—a reliable anchor in a storm of dreams.

A COMMITMENT TO PLAY

Tom's play *defines the world as play,* and his reality lies in his
commitment to play, not in the involuntary tendencies which
are often attributed to him. Actually Tom is in revolt against
nothing. To be sure, he feels the pinch of school and the discipline of Aunt Polly, but he has no sustained desire to escape
and no program of rebellion. What he does have is a perennial dream of himself as the hero and a commitment to the
dream which makes it come true not once, but as many times
as he can reorganize the village around his dream. The truth
the dream invariably comes to is *play*—a play which con-
verts all serious projects in the town to pleasure and at the
same time subverts all the adult rituals by revealing that actually they are nothing but dull play to begin with.

Thus in the famous whitewashing episode, the ritual of
the chore is converted into pleasure by Tom's stratagem.
And not simply converted, but shrewdly exploited by Tom.
To be sure, the episode discloses that Tom is an embryo
businessman and that he has a bright future in the society of
commerce and advertising, but such a criticism of Tom's
character ignores the essential criticism the episode itself
makes of the original chore. The chore was, after all, a kind
of dull-witted stratagem for getting work done at low pay in
the name of duty. Tom discovers—and surely it is a discovery worth making—that the task can be done four times as
thick and as well in the name of pleasure. Though Tom
shows off his handiwork he does no more than Aunt Polly
meant to do with him and the fence. . . .

The real audacity of *Tom Sawyer* is its commitment to the
pleasure principle. Though the book participates in parody,

burlesque, and satire, it clearly cannot be characterized by any of these terms. It is, after all, a tale—an *adventure*—and its commitment is not to exposing sham, as in the case of satire; nor is it to mocking a prior art form as in the case of parody and burlesque. Instead, the positive force—the force to which the world of St. Petersburg succumbs—is play itself.

Play is the reality principle in the book. What makes Tom Sawyer seem more real than the adults who submit to his power is his capacity to take his pleasure openly in the form of make-believe while they take theirs covertly under the guise of seriousness. Tom's virtue lies not in his good heart, his independence, or his pluck—none of which he really has—but in his truth to the pleasure principle which is the ultimate reality of the enchanted idyl. The very enchantment results from the indulgent perspective the author assumes toward the action. The narrator's indulgence is none other than the pleasure he takes in disclosing the play world.

The coupling of the outer pleasure with the inner world of play causes Tom's make-believe to seem true, whereas the adult "reality" and "duty" appear false and pretentious. This conversion, not so much process as point of view, is at once the humor and truth of the book. By inventing Tom Sawyer, Mark Twain had actually succeeded in dramatizing in a fictional narrative the possibilities of entertainment. He had projected through Tom Sawyer's imagination a world of boyhood in which play was the central reality, the defining value. The money Tom discovers in the cave in the final episode is a reward not for his courage or heroism—the indulgent perspective discloses his cowardice and essential self-love—but for his capacity to have dreamed it into reality with his make-believe imagination. And Tom quite characteristically appears before the townspeople to show off his treasure in one last exhibitionistic fling before the final curtain. The world of boyhood as it emerges in the pages of *Tom Sawyer* is a world where play, make-believe, and adventure are the living realities defining the false pieties and platitudes which constitute the dull pleasure of the adult world.

Mark Twain's invention of Tom Sawyer and his invention of the novel are thus one and the same thing. The reality principle of this first independent fiction is, as we have seen, play. The approach to fiction through the boy-character of a master player is an index to Mark Twain's inability to "believe" in conventional fiction. The exaggerated contempt in which he held fiction was his characteristic "humor" embodying his true perception. Mark Twain had no real use for conventional fiction because his entire genius—the "Mark Twain" in Samuel Clemens—had his being in the tall tale, a form which presented the truth as a lie, whereas the fiction he condemned presented the lie as the truth. That is why Mark Twain could say to Howells that he would not take Tom Sawyer into manhood because he "would just be like all the other one horse men in literature." Though he had promised in his conclusion to trace his figures into adult life, he never did; he could only call the changeless Tom Sawyer back on stage for more—and poorer—"acts."

In moving to the form of fiction, Mark Twain subverted the conventions of the form, not only by means of the burlesque and indulgent perspectives, but also through the character of Tom himself, whose "adventure" or plot is projected in terms of play and make-believe. The enchantment, the idyl, and the boy—the chief components of the book—create fiction as play instead of as truth. The book is no testimonial to the child's unfettered imagination transcending the materialism of the adult world. Instead, it creates existence under the name of pleasure, and portrays all human actions, no matter how "serious," as forms of play.

Tom Exploits St. Petersburg's Hypocrisy

Forrest G. Robinson

Forrest G. Robinson takes James Cox, author of the previous selection, to task in the following article. While Cox finds in *Tom Sawyer* a rejection of the dull world of adults in favor of an idyllic world of child's play, Forrest G. Robinson finds that Tom, in his artful plotting, follows the same complex, sophisticated rules as the adults do, and for the same reasons. Robinson contends that Tom collaborates with his neighbors in "bad faith," a reciprocal deception in which both sides pretend that social codes have not been violated. Besides his book *In Bad Faith: The Dynamics of Deception in Mark Twain's America*, from which this viewpoint is taken, Robinson has edited or co-edited two anthologies on Twain's work.

From that moment at the very beginning of *Tom Sawyer* when Aunt Polly looks over, rather than through, her spectacles, because "they were her state pair, the pride of her heart, and were built for 'style,' not service," we are alerted to the importance of social appearances in St. Petersburg. All of the important phases of village life are governed by ordinarily unspoken but evidently rigid rules and conventions. Domestic affairs, school, church, the political and legal establishments, the status hierarchy—in all of these areas a strict code works to enforce order and maintain "degree." For the most part, the members of the community have learned to accept, and even to take pleasure in, shaping themselves to the severely angular construction of their reality. The adults know their places in church, just as the children know theirs in school. All take parts, and play them, accepting apparent inconvenience and discomfort in the dutiful adherence to proper form. The young men of the community, for example, are willing to endure "sitting with their toes pressed against a wall for hours together" in order to achieve "the fashion of the day," boot toes turned sharply up "like sleigh-runners." Though the social regimen of the little society may strike us as comically extreme, our reaction is certainly in some degree the result of our failure—one we share with the residents of St. Petersburg—to recognize the constraints, objectively numerous and rather bizarre, that we bend to in our own daily lives. In larger part, we respond as we do because the novel directs our attention with unremitting persistence to the potent rigor of convention in the village society. Quite evidently, amidst his fretting about whether he was writing for adults or children, in *Tom Sawyer* Mark Twain yielded to a deep, though incompletely acknowledged, impulse to write a novel of social analysis.

Though the status hierarchy in St. Petersburg is rather rigidly fixed, the social ladder stretches generously from "the aged and needy postmaster, who had seen better days," through a broad range of middling families like the Sawyers and Harpers, to "the widow Douglas, fair, smart and forty," with her amiably aristocratic ways, and to such eminences as the "fine, portly, middle-aged gentleman with iron-gray hair . . . the great Judge Thatcher, brother of their own lawyer." The outcasts are surprisingly few. Huck Finn and Muff Potter are tolerated, and even granted condescending sympathy, so long as they keep their places on the margin. Only Injun Joe, half-breed and suspected felon, is forced completely outside the capacious orbit of local society. The great majority of the villagers accept their assigned ranks unreflectingly, without any apparent desire to resist the codes that order and limit their lives. Rather, they assert themselves through public display of conspicuous mastery of their roles. The necessity for spelling and spectacles and hymns is never questioned; thus the clear objective is to be the best speller, to wear the most fashionable spectacles, and, with the Rev. Mr. Sprague, to recite hymns "with a relish, in a peculiar style which was much admired in that part of the country." To be sure, the desire for approval occasionally reaches lunatic proportions. Consider the lamentable example of the young biblical enthusiast who once vaingloriously "spread himself" before the congregation by reciting from memory "three thousand verses without stopping." Unfortunately, "the strain upon his mental faculties was too great, and he was little better than an idiot from that day forth." In spite of such hazards, however, all St. Petersburg joins in the scramble for public acclaim. This is especially the case at church, where rituals of devotion and edification readily give way to an orgy of showing off. The superintendent, the librarian, the young men, the teachers, the boys and girls—members of every age and rank vie for attention. "And above it all" Judge Thatcher "sat and beamed a majestic judicial smile upon all the house, and warmed himself in the sun of his own grandeur— for he was 'showing off' too."

REINFORCING THE SOCIAL ORDER

Despite appearances, such wholesale self-indulgence reinforces rather than threatens the social order, for the ostentation is an expression of pride of place, not the ambition to subvert or climb. The showing off merely confirms the status quo. Following the urbanely superior narrator, the reader will undoubtedly be amused by the inflated posturings of the villagers; but he will be wrong if he supposes, as Cox does, that "the adult rituals" of St. Petersburg "are nothing but dull play."[1] We may find them dull, but only after we have enjoyed the show. More to the point, the villagers themselves take manifest pleasure in their relatively artless affectations. Hopelessly encumbered as they may appear, the members of the little community adhere to rigidly structured roles and routines with evident gusto. Our assessment of his style notwithstanding, the Rev. Mr. Sprague

> was regarded as a wonderful reader. At church "sociables" he was always called upon to read poetry; and when he was through, the ladies would lift up their hands and let them fall helplessly in their laps, and "wall" their eyes, and shake their heads, as much as to say, "Words cannot express it; it is too beautiful, *too* beautiful for this mortal earth."

These people have an enviable latitude and ingenuity when it comes to pleasure. Is it dull in the schoolmaster that he responds to news of a murder by declaring a "holiday for that afternoon"? Not in the view of his neighbors. Indeed, "the town would have thought strangely of him if he had not."

Cox's characterization of St. Petersburg features an extreme contrast between the real play of Tom Sawyer and the somehow inauthentic play of the adults. He equates Tom with the "world of boyhood ... where play, make-believe, and adventure are the living realities defining the false pieties and platitudes which constitute the dull pleasure of the adult world."[2] In addition to

---

1. James N. Cox, *Mark Twain: The Fate of Humor*, (Princeton, N.J.: Princeton University Press, 1966) p. 141 2. Ibid., p. 147

his misapprehension of adult amusements, Cox errs in both the breadth and the extremity of his definition of the "world of boyhood." The definition is too broad in that it ignores the vast majority of children in St. Petersburg who conform without protest to the values and behavior patterns prescribed by grownups. When we observe them at play, we find the children of St. Petersburg imitating their elders, holding "a juvenile court that was trying a cat for murder, in the presence of her victim, a bird." And if we remind ourselves of Sid and Mary Sawyer, of the Thatcher children and Amy Lawrence, of the impeccably dressed newcomer whom Tom scuffles with in Chapter I, of "the Model Boy, Willie Mufferson, taking as heedful care of his mother as if she were cut glass," of the scriptural prodigy who damages his brain, and of the nameless, obedient juvenile assemblage at school and church, then the "world of boyhood" shrinks dramatically.

TOM OBEYS ADULT MODELS OF CONDUCT

Cox's contrast is also too extreme in its clear suggestion that Tom inhabits a world of imagination and action that is radically different in degree, and possibly in kind, from the world of the grownups. The error here derives in good part, I believe, from limitations inherent in Cox's notion of play. He construes the term in the theatrical sense, with Tom cast as the central actor who performs before a receding audience composed of townspeople, the narrator (who handles props and draws the curtain), and a multitude of adoring readers. The advantages of this approach are very considerable, especially in opening up the pervasive theatricality of the novel's action and mode of presentation. But the method is misleading when it draws attention away from the fundamental realism of Mark Twain's social analysis, and when it leads to audience-response measurements of the alleged dullness of adult performances. In fact, Tom shows off like everyone else in town, and he does so for the same reasons, according to the same rules, and with the usual amount of zest and pleasure. Tom is willing, for example, to strive for excellence in spelling; but he extends himself at school principally because success earns him a "pewter medal which he had worn with ostentation for months." Moreover, there is abundant evidence that Tom advocates the strict observance of orderly, established procedures. "After the hymn had been sung," we learn, it was the convention for the minister to turn "himself into a bulletin board and read off 'notices' of

meetings and societies and things till it seemed that the list
would stretch out to the crack of doom." The narrator's amusement betrays a rather sharper edge when he observes, "Often,
the less there is to justify a traditional custom, the harder it is to
get rid of it." As if to add insult to injury, the minister goes on to
his regular, and regularly interminable, prayer for "the church,
and the little children of the church; . . . for the oppressed millions groaning under the heel of European monarchies and
Oriental despotisms" and "the heathen in the far islands of the
sea." We are hardly surprised to find that Tom "did not enjoy
the prayer, he only endured it—if he even did that much." But
despite the fact that he "was restive, all through it," Tom

> kept tally of the details of the prayer, unconsciously—for he was
> not listening, but he knew the ground of old, and the clergy-
> man's regular route over it—and when a little trifle of new mat-
> ter was interlarded, his ear detected it and his whole nature re-
> sented it; he considered additions unfair, and scoundrelly.

The reader may be inclined to share the narrator's view that
the prayer is mechanically prolix and therefore, like the
recital of "notices," somehow unjustified. For Tom, however,
the prayer is justified simply because it is "a traditional custom," and he objects to the slightest departure from its familiar, outward dullness. In this light, Tom's scrupulous adherence to literary "authorities" in his adventures, and his urging
Huck to submit to the widow's civilizing influence—"we can't
let you into the gang if you ain't respectable, you know"—
point to the unmistakably adult models which inform his values and conduct.[3]

PLAY VS. PLOTTING

We can move toward an even clearer sense of Tom's behavior if we shift briefly from the theatrical frame of reference
to a notion of play as spontaneous activity taking rise from

---

3. Early on in his chapter on *Tom Sawyer*, Cox acknowledges that the children imitate
the adults of St. Petersburg: "Tom Sawyer and his gang . . . are children at play—their
world is a play world in which adult rituals of love, death, war, and justice are reenacted in essentially harmless patterns" (131). He goes on to acknowledge that Tom
"has no sustained desire to escape" the constraints of village life, "and no program of
rebellion." In the same voice, however, Cox insists on a clear distinction between
Tom's "pleasure" and the adults' "dull play" (140–141). My general position on Tom's
relationship to the community, and some of its details, are clearly anticipated in Judith
Fetterley's fine essay, "The Sanctioned Rebel," *Studies in the Novel*, 3 (1971), 293–304.
Though she follows Cox in settling on a dramatic model for the analysis of Tom's role
in St. Petersburg, Fetterley stresses the similarities between the attitudes and behavior
of adults and children (300–301), and argues that the townspeople endure Tom's ego-
tism and aggressiveness because he amuses them and affirms their values. "For indeed the focus of *The Adventures of Tom Sawyer* is on the harmony between Tom and
his community and on the satisfactions of the symbiotic relationship between them"
(303).

the relatively unencumbered promptings of the imagination.[4] The nearest approach to such "free" play occurs at the beginning of the famous whitewashing episode, when Ben Rogers appears on the scene [pretending to be a steamboat]. . . .

Meanwhile, apparently absorbed in his own activity, Tom goes on with the whitewashing, and "paid no attention to the steamboat." In fact, however, and in contrast to Ben's total oblivion to his actual surroundings, Tom is alive to the possibilities of the objective circumstances. While Ben plays at being a steamboat, Tom plays—in a very different way—at seeming not to notice. On one side, we have virtually unselfconscious make-believe; on the other, alert, self-conscious and purposive dissimulation. While Ben plays, Tom schemes. In the upshot, of course, artless play succumbs to artful plotting.

In following the inevitable logic of the child- versus adult-play argument, Cox is inclined to minimize what he calls the "embryo businessman" in Tom, and focuses instead on "the essential criticism the episode . . . makes of the original chore." Viewed from this angle, the whitewashing incident exposes the poverty of adult initiative—Aunt Polly's demands are a "dull-witted stratagem for getting work done at low pay in the name of duty"—and the concomitant superiority of a juvenile rejoinder in which "Tom shows off his handiwork" while completing the task "in the name of pleasure."[5] In thus preserving his critical line of thought, however, Cox ignores the force of the contrast between Tom and Ben, and seriously overstates the contrast between the behavior of Aunt Polly and Tom. If we acknowledge—as I think we must—that the episode demonstrates Tom's prodigious mastery of deception and the strategies of self-interest, then we must go on to observe that his conduct, unlike Ben's, is hardly spontaneous and free. In fact, if it is true that Aunt Polly contrives to get "work done at low pay," then the same can be said of Tom, except that he gets it done at a considerable profit to himself, and that the name of pleasure serves his purposes better than "duty.". . .

COLLABORATING IN BAD FAITH

In winning his way to the top, Tom outwits and exploits members from every age group and class in the community.

4. Cox seems to have something like this in mind when he asserts that "in Mark Twain's world of boyhood, the imagination represents the capacity for mimicry, impersonation, make-believe, and play"; *Mark Twain: The Fate of Humor*, p. 148 5. Ibid., p. 141

The other children are twice taken in, and provide ready sources of free labor and capital. The adults are equally easy prey; for, as Tom shrewdly divines, their incredulity is not as deep as their craving for amusement. Along the way, Tom makes a mockery of honesty and good faith; but he does so in a manner that is, paradoxically, easily detected and yet imperious to public disapproval. We can begin to unravel this paradox by observing that in moving toward his objectives, Tom has enjoyed the cooperation, both willing and unwilling, of the community. His victims either get what they asked for, or have themselves to blame for their undoing, or both. In effect, Tom has collaborated with his neighbors in "bad faith," the reciprocal deception of self and other, generally in the denial of departures from public codes of correct behavior. A telling feature of such acts is their incorporation of silent prohibitions against the admission that they have occurred. For their part, Tom's neighbors can never fully acknowledge to themselves or others the full extent to which they have been deceived. To do so would risk a humiliating revelation of their willingness to be misled. On Tom's part, full acknowledgment of bad faith would entail the potential for an unbearable assault of guilt, or the loss, through their public disclosure, of the social intuitions which form the basis of his power. This delicate equipoise of threats to the collective peace of mind would collapse were it not for the fact that bad faith is the ruling characteristic in the social dynamics of the village.

St. Petersburg society is a complex fabric of lies: of half-truths, of simulation, dissimulation, broken promises, exaggeration, and outright falsehoods. Tom is exceptional only in the sheer quantity of his showing off; Huck's faith is more than once betrayed; the local ladies are easy marks for vendors of quack cure-alls and exotic religions; the entire community turns a blind eye to Injun Joe's grave robbing and the presence of liquor in the Temperance Tavern; and the Judge himself is moved to deliver an encomium on lies of the generous, magnanimous stripe. One imagines, in fact, that St. Petersburg is hardly unusual in all this, and that varieties of bad faith are universally a feature of complex societies. They are the covert mechanisms of flexibility and resilience that work imperceptibly to mitigate rigid customs and laws, and thus provide a measure of latitude adequate to the accommodation of apparently incompatible demands for conformity and individual self-expression. As I am using the term, then, "bad faith" describes the spectrum of unacknowledged and sublimated deceits that a society tolerates as the price of stability and equanimity. It is the "give" in the outwardly stiff St. Petersburg system.

It must be obvious by now that if Tom is playing at all, he is playing a sustained, purposeful, relatively complex social game. His success is the index of his masterful mimicry of adult strategies, and of his possession, to an uncommon degree, of social intuition, audacity, and an arsenal of artifice. Their skillful use enables him to gain glittering notoriety and the pinnacle of the social ladder, and at the same time to avoid censure. But if Tom is like Icarus in his mastery of artifice and in the swiftness and dizzying pitch of his ascent, he is Icarian as well in his precipitous vulnerabilities. Tom's genius for manipulation makes it possible for him to play at the perilous margins of social tolerance for bad faith. As we have seen, the potential for exploitation is great; but susceptible as he is to the pride of mastery, Tom is prone to the kind of false move that threatens a fall as abrupt as his climb. The radical extremes of Tom's potential are precisely, if somewhat obliquely, evident to those villagers "that believed he would be President, yet, if he escaped hanging."

THE KEY TO TOM'S POWER

Tom's outward vulnerability to his neighbors has its inward counterpart in his vulnerability to himself. The indispensable key to Tom's power is his unique, even transcendent, intuitive grasp of the mechanisms of bad faith that govern behavior in St. Petersburg. The other villagers are all but blind to their immersion in the quotidian round of deceit, and thus complacently unaware of what we might be inclined, in a righteous mood, to call their hypocrisy. Indeed, it is the essential first article of bad faith that its agents live in the illusion that they are virtually free of the impulse to deceive or be deceived. Thus the local residents, fully and unconsciously acculturated as they are, deceive themselves and each other without frequent or significant misgivings. For Tom, however, the correlative to enhanced social acuity is heightened vulnerability to a crippling double consciousness. On one side, Tom recognizes and subscribes to the overt code of his community. On the other, he is the possessor of a profound subliminal insight into the dynamics of the social game. But this insight is an asset only so long as it works below the threshold of consciousness; for full self-awareness would be accompanied by the onset of guilt and the collapse of manipulative social power. At some sub-merged level, Tom knows that he cannot afford to know what he knows. Thus he is obliged to expend large sums of psychic energy in the abridgment of self-knowledge. As we shall see, though he is generally successful in this enter-prise, he is never completely out of danger of an upsurge of painful emotion from beneath the surface of conscious-ness. . . .

The novel's failure to fully resolve Tom's dilemma is the price Mark Twain paid for the preservation of his fictional point of view. For if Tom's intuitive manipulation of perva-sive bad faith produces both plotting and plot, the same per-ception in the reader, issuing from our privileged view of Tom's intrigues, produces humor. It follows, of course, that the key to the novel's humorous consistency of tone is the narrator's ability to preserve his good-natured condescen-sion to the villagers' double standards. On those occasions when his superior detachment from village eccentricity gives way to anger at perceived hypocrisy, we are reminded of Tom's dilemma and made aware of the fine line that sep-arates humor from the angriest variety of social satire.

An Idealized Relationship Between Individual and Community

Thomas Blues

Mark Twain sought to create an impossible situation in *Tom Sawyer*, writes Thomas Blues of the University of Kentucky. He tried to make Tom an independent individual who challenges a community's values and disrupts the social order, who is nonetheless welcome, even when he triumphs over the community. Although this would be an unlikely outcome in real life, Blues notes that Twain bends the fictional world to his will.

In this essay I attempt to demonstrate how Mark Twain's complex attitudes toward the relation of the individual to the community influence the meaning and direction of his fiction. My fundamental argument is that at the center of Mark Twain's consciousness as a novelist was a vision of an idealized relation between the individual and the community, in which an independent individual could freely challenge the community's values, disrupt its sense of order, and yet somehow retain his identity as a conventional member of it. An impossible ideal, no doubt, and fraught with tensions that Mark Twain could not ultimately control; yet it underlies the structures and themes of each novel he wrote up to and including *Adventures of Huckleberry Finn*. . . .

Difficult as it is to define precisely, the term *community* as I apply it to this study should be explained. Early and late, Mark Twain instinctively chose small towns as settings in his fiction. Even in his late fiction, when he vilified society at large ("the damned human race") he tended to objectify the target of his criticism as the town. St. Petersburg, Daw-

son's Landing, Camelot, Hadleyburg, Eseldorf—these towns
are more than mere geographical or political loci; they exist
as social entities (defined by their embodiment of a complex
cluster of official values and attitudes) and serve to subsume
their individual inhabitants into a collective role of oppo-
nent, conscience, and audience for Mark Twain's protago-
nists. It is in the attempt to evoke this sense of the town as
social organism operating as fictional antagonist that I use
the term. . . .

TOM SAWYER'S CONFLICT WITH THE COMMUNITY

The conflict between the individual and the community is
sharply defined and ingeniously resolved in Mark Twain's . . .
Tom Sawyer. For Tom not only wants to make his dreams
come true in the real world, he wants to be applauded by the
adult community for violating its stability.

Walter Blair has argued that Tom Sawyer is "a working out
in fictional form of a boy's maturing." He bases his thesis on
the supposition that "every subplot in the book eventuates in
an expression of adult approval."[1] But Tom's triumphs are
made possible by Mark Twain's transformation of an adult
community into one very much resembling a world of children. In granting Tom his triumphs without endangering either the town or his standing in it, Mark Twain furnished him
with a community that applauded its victimizer and was more
than willing to regard victimization as a virtue.

RESHAPING THE ADULT WORLD

The novel early provides two important indicators of Tom's
notion of a dominant relation to the adult community and of
Mark Twain's method of protecting him from the conse-
quences of its realization. The first, Tom's pirate fantasy,
should be treated as an expression of genuine aggression. Although he has no serious intentions of terrorizing St. Petersburg by main force, he gains by fraud and guile the quality of
submission he desires in his daydream: "he would suddenly
appear at the old village and stalk into church, brown and
weather-beaten, in his black velvet doublet and trunks, his
great jack-boots, his crimson sash, his belt bristling with
horse-pistols, his crime-rusted cutlass at his side, his slouch
hat with waving plumes, his black flag unfurled, with the skull

1. "On the Structure of *Tom Sawyer,*" *Modern Philology,* XXXVII (Aug. 1939), pp. 84–85

and cross-bones on it, and hear with swelling ecstasy the whisperings, 'it's Tom Sawyer the Pirate!—the Black Avenger of the Spanish Main!'" As Tom strives to realize his dream he risks alienating himself from the town, but Mark Twain reduces the adult world to make his performances seem innocent and entertaining diversions.

The second indicator, the famous whitewashing scene, is a capsule demonstration of how Mark Twain reshapes the community to fit Tom's imaginative dimensions of it. The scene begins with Aunt Polly vowing to turn Tom's "Saturday holiday into captivity at hard labor." Tom quickly abandons self-pity and beguiles the "free boys" into paying him for the privilege of painting the fence. But Aunt Polly is the most important link in his chain of victims. Impressed with what she supposes is his diligence, she gives him an apple and a "lecture upon the added value and flavor a treat took to itself when it came without sin through virtuous effort."

A VICTORY OVER CONSCIENCE

Little is at stake in the whitewashing episode, but the pattern of Tom's first triumph is repeated on a more serious scale in the flight to Jackson's Island and back. For Tom returns to convince an entire adult community that a cruel hoax is fun and to persuade Aunt Polly that it is actually a virtuous act. The Black Avenger and his friends find that leaving town is one thing, breaking with it something else. After the initial excitement of camping out and watching the townspeople search for their bodies had worn off, the boys "could not keep back thoughts of certain persons at home who were not enjoying this fine frolic as much as they were." Anxious to remain on the island and at the same time maintain a conscience-clear relationship with his home, Tom returns at night to leave a reassuring note; it reads, *"We ain't dead— we are only off being pirates.'"* From a hiding place in his house Tom listens to the conversation and "was sufficiently touched by his aunt's grief to long to rush out from under the bed and overwhelm her with joy—and the theatrical gorgeousness of the thing appealed strongly to his nature, too, but he resisted and lay still." Tom learns that the funeral will be held the following Sunday—four days hence—and when Aunt Polly goes to bed he almost leaves the note. "His heart was full of pity for her. He took out his sycamore scroll and placed it by the candle. But something occurred to him, and he lingered considering. His face lighted with a happy solution of his thought; he put the bark hastily in his pocket." Tom's victory over conscience clears the way for his sensational return to the town.

Actually, his intention to appear alive at his own funeral serves two purposes. Next day on Jackson's Island Tom staves off mutiny by promising his homesick gang a glorious return if they will hold out for a few more days. Having won his boys over, Tom completes his triumph on a larger scale in St. Petersburg three days later. True to his pirate fantasy Tom returns to a crowded church. The minister urges the startled assembly into a hymn of joyful thanksgiving, and "As the 'sold' congregation trooped out they said they would almost be willing to be made ridiculous again to hear Old Hundred sung like that once more."

Aunt Polly is not so readily won over; she does not think it was such "'a fine joke . . . to keep everybody suffering 'most a week.'" But her hesitancy is grist for Tom's mill. First he tells his aunt he returned in a dream to console her. When that story is exposed he tells her of his actual return, of the suppressed note, and a half-truth about the purpose of the clandestine visit: "'I wanted to keep you from grieving— that was all that made me come.'" She accepts the story as a forgivable lie—"'it was such good-heartedness in him to tell it'"—and when she finds the note in Tom's jacket she vows she "'could forgive the boy, now, if he'd committed a million sins!'" Her sentimentality leads her to obscure a sterner truth. Anxious to believe in Tom's essential virtue, Aunt Polly finds it in a cruel and deliberate hoax.

EMOTIONAL EXCESS OF THE ADULT COMMUNITY

Aunt Polly's emotional excess, however, is typical of that of the adult community at large. Albert E. Stone says that Tom is essentially a passive character "subservient in the main to the adult schedule of events,"[2] but he fails to consider that Tom's triumphs over the community are possible only because he can depend upon its hysterical and childish reactions to his antics. The Jackson's Island hoax is but the first of four episodes in which the townspeople demonstrate their inability to distinguish between a genuinely heroic action

2. Albert E. Stone, Jr., *The Innocent Eye: Childhood in Mark Twain's Imagination* (New Haven, 1961), pp. 79–80

and a vulgar bid for the limelight. Nor can they react to either except with sensational emotional display.

Tom's return from the island reinvolves him in an unsettled moral problem—his silence in the face of Muff Potter's

---

BECOMING A HERO BY FOOLING THE PUBLIC

In his Autobiography, *Twain recalled a mesmerizer who visited Hannibal for several performances. Twain was* "fourteen or fifteen years old, the age at which a boy is willing to endure all things, suffer all things short of death by fire, if thereby he may be conspicuous and show off before the public; and so, when I saw the 'subjects' perform their foolish antics on the platform and make the people laugh and shout and admire I had a burning desire to be a subject myself." *Twain pretended to be* "mesmerized," *or hypnotized, and gradually began to improve upon the* "professor's" *instructions, which were intended to prove he was under the man's spell. The excerpt below describes the crowd's response to a particularly audacious prank, when he pretended to stalk a bully with a gun. (The performer claimed that whatever the boy had done was in direct and correct response to his* "silent" *instructions.)*

There was a storm of applause, and the magician, addressing the house, said, most impressively—

"That you may know how really remarkable this is and how wonderfully developed a subject we have in this boy, I assure you that without a single spoken word to guide him he has carried out what I mentally commanded him to do, to the minutest detail. I could have stopped him at a moment in his vengeful career by mere exertion of my will, therefore the poor fellow who has escaped was at no time in danger."

So I was not in disgrace. I returned to the platform a hero and happier than I have ever been in this world since. As regards mental suggestion, my fears of it were gone. I judged that in case I failed to guess what the professor might be willing me to do, I could count on putting up something that would answer just as well. I was right, and exhibitions of unspoken suggestion became a favorite with the public. Whenever I perceived that I was being willed to do something I got up and did something—anything that occurred to me—and the magician, not being a fool, always ratified it. When people asked me, "How *can* you tell what he is willing you to do?" I said, "It's just as easy," and they always said admiringly, "Well, it beats *me* how you can do it."

The Autobiography of Mark Twain, edited by Charles Neider. New York: Harper, 1959.

certain conviction for a crime he did not commit. Having witnessed Injun Joe's murder of Dr. Robinson, Tom and Huck Finn vowed silence for fear of the half-breed's reprisal. Tom's conscience increasingly nags him as the trial date draws closer, but he manages to live with his guilt until he can reveal the truth to a packed courtroom. One remembers that Tom had earlier hesitated until the most dramatic moment to take Becky Thatcher's punishment for a ripped anatomy book and that she had praised his nobility; now an even more startling revelation captures a larger adoration. The courtroom audience "hung upon his words, taking no note of time, rapt in the ghastly fascinations of the tale." His story makes Tom "a glittering hero once more—the pet of the old, the envy of the young." The fact that Muff Potter has waited in agony for months to hang for a crime he is innocent of is forgotten.

When Tom returns from the dead a second time, after his ordeal with Becky Thatcher in the cave, the town enjoys not a moment of quiet thankfulness but a gaudy parade: "the population massed itself and moved toward the river, met the children coming in an open carriage drawn by shouting citizens, thronged around it, joined its homeward march, and swept magnificently up the main street roaring huzzah after huzzah!" Tom's final triumph is his dramatic display of the treasure to the citizens assembled to honor Huck Finn. This last sensation steals the scene from Huck and nearly enervates the town: "It was talked about, gloated over, glorified, until the reason of many of the citizens tottered under the strain of the unhealthy excitement."

AN EXCESSIVELY BENEVOLENT COMMUNITY

At the end of the novel Tom successfully persuades Huck Finn to return to the Widow Douglas's home. His argument is that respectability and new wealth "'ain't going to keep me back from turning robber.'" Professor Blair views this as the culmination of Tom's growing up, his capitulation to the "enemy."[3] But in fact the opposite is true. Tom's claim that he can at once maintain membership in the respectable adult community and continue his career as its victimizer is valid pre-

3. Blair, "On the Structure of *Tom Sawyer*," p. 88. Robert Regan, who has also noticed the "theatrical artificiality" of the town, accepts Blair's thesis but argues that Tom in the final chapter is "a relapsed juvenile" whose major goal is leadership of the other boys. See *Unpromising Heroes: Mark Twain and His Characters* (Berkeley and Los Angeles, 1966), pp. 126–30.

cisely because the town has never failed to come over to his side. Mark Twain provides Tom Sawyer with a community which willingly capitulates to his selfish desires for awed and reverent attention, a community which reacts with excessive benevolence to whatever he does. Though his depredations are potentially destructive, no permanent harm ever comes to those who bear the burden of his imagination.

A Rite of Passage

Kenneth S. Lynn

Tom Sawyer's attempts to free himself from confinement and move toward romantic freedom are resolved by the grim experience of being trapped in the cave with Becky and the murderous Injun Joe, writes Kenneth S. Lynn, Lovejoy Professor of History, emeritus, at Johns Hopkins University. After the three-day dreamlike experience underground, which Lynn sees as a ceremony of induction, Tom emerges ready to take his place as a respectable member of the community. Besides his book on Twain, from which this viewpoint is excerpted, Lynn has also written on Twain's close friend and editor William Dean Howells.

No American writer, past or present, has ever surpassed the extraordinary vividness of Mark Twain's evocations of the Happy Valley of his childhood. Twain's achievement rests primarily on two things, the power of his literary style and the shrewdness of his psychological insight into the minds of children. But style and insight were in turn the outgrowths of love, a love of amazing intensity for the Hannibal, Missouri, of his youth.

To think of Hannibal, Twain once wrote, was like "bathing in the Fountain of Youth.". . . If he was nostalgic about Hannibal, it was not because the town had been part of a better America of long ago, but because Hannibal represented the world of his childhood. Like the Garden of Eden, the Hannibal of Twain's memory stood outside of time altogether, insulated from the taint and the tragedy of history by the magic circle of youth.

Viewed as a continuous history, Twain's early travel books show a lonely American backtrailing in time toward that magic circle. In *The Adventures of Tom Sawyer*, the long voyage home is over; Twain's persona is now a boy in Paradise.

Excerpted from *Mark Twain and Southwestern Humor*, by Kenneth S. Lynn. Copyright © 1959 by Kenneth S. Lynn. Reprinted with the author's permission.

The choice of a fictional name for heavenly Hannibal was perhaps inevitable: St. Peters-burg. Just why he settled on a third-person narrative, instead of the first-person style that had previously served him well, is not, however, so easily understandable, and there is reason to believe that he ultimately regretted his decision. . . . Deciding, too, that his persona had become too fictitious a character to be called "Mark Twain" any longer, he hit upon Tom Sawyer as an appropriate substitute, a name that would be echoed in "Villagers of 1840–3," an unpublished autobiographical reminiscence of Hannibal written during the '90s, in which Twain gave the Clemens family the pseudonym of Carpenter.

Despite the changes in name and point of view, the child in the Happy Valley is nevertheless the same lonesome character whom we have met before [in Twain's earlier works]. If the narrator of *The Innocents Abroad* jokingly described himself as a "helpless orphan," Tom Sawyer is precisely that. And not only is Tom being brought up by a woman who is not his mother, but he believes that Aunt Polly loves his half-brother Sid more than she does him. Tom feels himself further disaffected, not only from Aunt Polly but from the whole community, by his youthful high spirits. Whereas Sid and Mary are fond of going to church, Tom hates it "with his whole heart." There is a "restraint about whole clothes and cleanliness that galled him"; and he envies lawless Huck Finn because the river waif does not have to go to school or call any human being master. Phrases like "away off" and "far off" recur frequently in the novel, signifying the boy's wish to escape to the drifting river, or to the "soft green sides" of Cardiff Hill, to go somewhere, in fine, far beyond "the reach of capture and punishment." Throughout the novel, we are presented with two realities—the prosaic reality of the town, and the fantastic reality of Tom Sawyer's imagination—and the boy continually strives to escape from the former to the latter, with the result that the movement from realistic confinement to romantic freedom utterly dominates the action. Thus the voice of restrictive authority, as symbolized by Aunt Polly, is heard in the very first word of the book—"Tom!"—and in the ensuing chapter Tom twice makes a bolt for freedom. The first time he does, Aunt Polly seizes him as he bolts from a dark hiding-place toward the light and freedom of outdoors, but he scares her and gets away. A page or so later, he flees the supper table to escape her wrath at his having played hooky and gone swimming. The chapter culminates, however, as it had begun, with the reassertion of the confinement idea, as Aunt Polly decides to turn the boy's Saturday holiday into "captivity at hard labor."

But in St. Petersburg, inside the magic circle of childhood, familiar feelings of disaffection and fears of confinement have been turned into child's play in a garden. Tom is only half-serious about his rebellion, just as Aunt Polly is merely half-hearted about her punishment of the boy. To put it another way, an indulgent St. Petersburg permits a boy to "run away" without his ever having to leave home—which is why the place is so heavenly. Rebellion, alienation, and flight are muted and contained in *Tom Sawyer* within a larger framework of acceptance and connection. Partaking in many ways of the quality of a dream, Tom Sawyer is a story of wish-fulfillments, in which the hero's most fantastic imaginings are made flesh and the pleasure principle reigns triumphant.

SUBVERTING FRANKLIN'S VIRTUES

In the first of the notable wish-fulfillments of the novel, the "hard labor" of whitewashing the fence is transmuted into a glorious game; by a dreamlike inversion of the maxims of [Ben Franklin's] Poor Richard, laziness becomes the way to wealth. One need go no further than Twain's essay, "The Late Benjamin Franklin," to realize how much the author of *Tom Sawyer* cherished that inversion. Poor Richard's maxims were full of animosity toward boys, in Twain's opinion, and in making that statement he had in mind certain private memories as well as public observations. For Mark Twain not only shared Joel Chandler Harris's general misgivings about the narrowness and imaginative sterility of a business civilization, he had seen what Poor Richard's philosophy had done to his brother Orion, that hapless incompetent who made his life miserable by following Franklin's dietary and timesaving rules in the belief that proper habits would make him rich, and who had once operated a thoroughly unsuccessful printing establishment named, with pathetic optimism, the Ben Franklin Print Shop. If Twain was himself given to writing self-help letters to his brother, he was also capable of taking off Orion's devotion to *The Way to Wealth* in an essay called "Advice to Youth," in which he advised young men to get up with the lark, and then train the lark to get up at half-past nine, etc. Similarly, in "Autobiography of

a Damned Fool" he told of how he had once modeled himself on the rigorous regimen described in Franklin's *Autobiography* by taking a cold swim every morning, until one day
a thief stole his clothes while he was in the water and he
nearly died of exposure. Perhaps his most succinct opinion
of Franklin was rendered in "3000 Years Among the Mi-
crobes," where he introduced the pride of Philadelphia in
the guise of a yellow fever germ. The whitewashing episode
in *Tom Sawyer*, however, is Twain's most prodigious piece of
anti-Franklinism. In its portrayal of a gloriously relaxed
Tom allowing his friends to pay him for the privilege of
painting the fence for him, the scene comically illustrates
the thesis that neither work nor the appearance of work is
necessary for success. In *Roughing It*, Twain's hero had as-
pired to easy wealth, but failed to attain it; in the wish-
fulfillment-world of *Tom Sawyer*, he succeeds.

TRANSMUTING DEATH INTO CHILD'S PLAY

Following this triumphant scene, the metronomic rhythm of
the novel, with its movement from confinement to freedom
and back again, begins to describe more drastic arcs.
Slapped sprawling to the floor by Aunt Polly for a crime he
has not committed, Tom flees to the river's edge where, in a
manner reminiscent of the death-fascinated narrators of *The
Innocents* and *Roughing It*, he sits contemplating the "dreary
vastness of the stream, wishing, the while, that he could only
be drowned, all at once and unconsciously, without under-
going the uncomfortable routine devised by nature." Like all
other wishes, Tom's death-wish is soon granted to him, but
again the grimness of adult reality is transmuted into child's
play. Tom desires to "die *temporarily*," and the sojourn on
Jackson's Island with Huck Finn and Joe Harper, culminat-
ing in the boys' dramatic appearance at their own funeral,
fully meets the morbid requirements of his puerile imagination. As in the scene of the beautiful sunrise on Jackson's Island that follows upon the terrific, nocturnal thunderstorm
which has all but torn the island apart, the sun is always
shining the next morning in Tom Sawyer's world. Nothing
serious has really happened; indeed, nothing at all seems to
have happened, for time in *Tom Sawyer* appears to stand
perfectly still. The beautiful woods and fields, the magnificent river, the pretty, white-painted town, sleep peacefully in
the eternal Missouri summer. The action of the novel takes

place some time in the 1840s, but the booming of the guns along the Rio Grande is not heard in the Happy Valley; when Senator Benton comes to town to speak, no report is given of what he said; in hermetic St. Petersburg there is not the least hint of the slavery crisis, or of an oncoming civil war. . . . St. Petersburg is a morally immaculate society, and *Tom Sawyer* is "simply a hymn," as Mark Twain said, "put into prose form to give it a worldly air"—a hymn sung in honor and glory of the possibility of American innocence.

Evil appears in St. Petersburg only in the person of a social outcast who is both a criminal and a colored man: Injun Joe. When, having played Robin Hood in the woods with Joe Harper, Tom trudges off home, "grieving that there were no outlaws any more, and wondering what modern civilization could claim to have done to compensate for their loss," events are as usual conspiring to satisfy his wishes in the very next chapter. In the graveyard in the dead of night, Tom and Huck come upon . . . a respected doctor of the town stealing a body from a grave. The sight terrifies the boys, but it produces no further reaction. . . . Tom Sawyer is not disillusioned or made cynical by what he has seen. Terror does not lead him on to any disturbing speculations about Dr. Robinson, or about doctors in general, or about the possibility of moral hypocrisy in respectable St. Petersburg. Huck is equally unwilling to consider the possibility of corruption in Eden; as is true of his discovery later in the book that the Temperance tavern in the town is a cover-up for a whisky hell, he passes off the revelation of Dr. Robinson's true character without a comment. Tom and Huck's attention in the graveyard is not fixed on Dr. Robinson, the respectable authority-figure, but on the vicious outcast who murders him. The dangers of social disillusionment are thus bypassed, and the nightmare has no significance beyond its own enthralling horror. Far from puncturing Tom Sawyer's dreamworld, grim reality has simply enlivened it. Tom Sawyer in the graveyard has merely had another marvelous good time, flirting with death and getting away with it.

THE CAVE AS A SOURCE OF TRANSFORMATION

Throughout the novel Tom also flirts with Becky Thatcher, his schoolgirl sweetheart. At the end of the novel, the two flirtations—with love and with death—come together in the episode of the cave. It is the first underground adventure in

Twain's work in which the significance of the experience of going under the earth, the effect of it on the hero's life, is made dramatically plain. As in E.M. Forster's *A Passage to India*, the cave in *Tom Sawyer* is a source of transforming experience, except that instead of upsetting things it resolves them, once and for all, and brings the novel's alternating movement between confinement and escape to an end.

In staging the climax of his novel, Mark Twain drew directly on his personal experience, for he himself had played in caves all through his childhood. As any boy who has grown up in limestone country knows, caves can provide endless enchantment to a youthful imagination. Joseph G. Baldwin, exploring the Virginia countryside in his youth, came to know a certain cave near Staunton, where, according to legend, a bag of bones had been found shortly after an Englishman living in the neighborhood had mysteriously disappeared. A doctor in the town had fallen under suspicion for a time, but he swore that the bones were the remains of a Negro corpse which he had dissected, and nothing more was done about the case. A doctor in Hannibal also contributed to the dark magic of the caves that young Sam Clemens knew. Dr. McDowell, a surgeon, rumored to be a body-snatcher like the Dr. Robinson of *Tom Sawyer*, had stored arms in one of the caves outside the town in hopeful preparation for an invasion of Mexico. Even more bizarrely, McDowell had also buried his dead daughter in a cave, placing the corpse of the fourteen-year-old girl in a copper cylinder filled with alcohol, and submerging the cylinder in a subterranean spring. The top of the cylinder being removable, young bucks of the town were given to hauling it up to the surface of the water and unscrewing the top for a look at the face of death. A further source of enchantment was the widely held belief that the Murrell gang had buried a chest of gold in one of the caves near Hannibal. Is it any wonder that Mark Twain should have confided to his notebook that in dreams "everything is more deep and strong and sharp and real than is ever its pale imitation in the unreal life which is ours when we go about awake and clotted with our artificial selves," and that when he dreamed he was apt to go wandering into caves?

In the cave episode in *Tom Sawyer*, elements of Twain's personal experience are combined and outlandishly rearranged, as if by a trick of faulty memory, or as in a dream.

Injun Joe, the murderer of the body-snatcher, has buried guns and gold in McDougal's (not McDowell's) cave; in its subterranean depths, death comes in search of the young girl, Becky Thatcher, and of Tom as well.

To this fantastic place Tom Sawyer has come in hope, as always, of adventure. In company with Becky, he breaks away from his fellow picnickers to look for the romance and freedom of the unknown; passing through "The Drawing-Room," "The Cathedral," and "Aladdin's Palace," he and Becky wander down into the cave's nameless and "secret depths." Once, much earlier in the book, Tom had persuaded Becky to kiss him; later they had quarreled when he discovered her looking at a naked figure in the schoolmaster's anatomy book; now, however, holding hands as they walk along, and awed by the sights of an underground anatomy book—by "shining stalactites of the length and circumference of a man's leg," and by "a subterranean lake . . . which stretched its dim length away until its shape was lost in the shadows"—they draw more intimately together than ever before. When awe gives way to fear of the cave's bottomless mystery, Tom puts his arm around her and she buries her face in his bosom. When they eat a piece of cake saved from the picnic, Becky says, "It's our wedding-cake, Tom."

BELOW THE BOUNDS OF HEAVEN

All the while that they are descending, they are also growing more fatigued. As drowsiness overtakes them, they fall asleep for long periods. When they go on again, it is as if they are walking in their sleep. The entire experience becomes more and more like a dream, so that when Tom encounters Injun Joe far down in the bowels of the cave, the boy does not logically question why or how the outlaw should be there, or if he is mistaking an illusion for reality. He accepts the Indian's incongruous appearance with all the conviction that one accepts incongruities in dreams. In *Tom Sawyer*, as in the fiction of Twain's literary idol, Cervantes, the cave is the dwelling-place of fantastically unreal creatures who yet compel belief. Pancracio, the deceived husband in one of Cervantes' *Interludes*, is frightened by devils who supposedly live in the caves of Salamanca, while Don Quixote in the cave of Montesinos thinks he sees the sleeping heroes of a golden past. Tom Sawyer's romantic imagination is equally willing to accept the impossible, but the joke in Tom's case reverses the typical Cervantean situation in that the dream-apparition turns out to be real. Covered with black mud, Tom had once masqueraded as an Indian; had boasted of taking a thousand white scalps. Now, far down in McDougal's cave, he finds himself involved in a far grimmer game with an Indian nightmarishly disguised as a white man. For once in his life, Tom has strayed beyond—or below—the bounds of Heaven; he has stepped across the limits of safety into a subterranean vault where death threatens to become more than a temporary condition. Terrified, the boy turns and runs—and the direction in which he flees is back where he came from.

REBIRTH

Having descended into the cave, Tom and Becky spend there a Biblical total of three days and nights. At the end of that time, they crawl up a long tunnel toward the light and are "reborn," after having been given up for dead. From the moment that he reappears, Tom is a changed person. He was not the Model Boy of the village when he went into the cave, nor is he when he comes out. He still is, and remains so throughout *Huckleberry Finn*, a prankster. But he is no longer even half-serious about running away. At the end of the novel, it is Huck who speaks of "cussed smothery houses," not Tom, while the ingenious plans for playing pirate and Indian games with which Tom had once persuaded Huck and Joe Harper to prolong their escapade on Jackson's Island are now employed by Tom as a bribe to tempt Huck into living at the Widow Douglas's and becoming respectable. To be a member of the outlaw gang Tom now forms does not mean that one is at war with the community; indeed, it means just the reverse. Pleading to join on his own terms, Huck says, "Now Tom, hain't you always ben friendly to me? You wouldn't shet me out, would you, Tom? You wouldn't do that, now, *would* you, Tom?" But Tom is adamant: "Huck, I wouldn't want to, and I don't want to—but what would people say? Why, they'd say, 'Mph! Tom Sawyer's Gang! pretty low characters in it!' They'd mean you, Huck." The seemingly unconnected events of the long Missouri summer have conformed, we see now, to a ritualistic pattern; the semi-rebellion of Tom Sawyer has in fact been the means of initiating him into the tribe, and his symbolic death in the cave, occurring as it does at the end of his probation, effectively concludes the ceremony of induction.

With his rebirth, Tom's life becomes more definite. The money he has discovered in the cave is put out for him at a tidy six per cent return; so settled is the fact that Becky is Tom's girl that one might almost suppose they had reached a definite understanding; when Judge Thatcher tells Tom he has high hopes of his becoming a great lawyer or a great soldier someday we cannot doubt the Judge's judgment. If the book does not follow Tom into manhood—for if it did, Twain said, then his hero would become a liar just like all the other "one-horse men in literature"—Tom nevertheless accepts the adult universe more fully than ever before. In embracing St. Petersburg and its values, he draws the magic circle of childhood about the entire society, thus reaffirming the incorruptible innocence of the heavenly town that Twain remembered from his youth. Of all Twain's major fictions, *Tom Sawyer* is the only one in which an initiation ends neither in flight nor in catastrophe, but in serene and joyous acceptance.

CHAPTER 3

Themes in *Tom Sawyer*

READINGS ON
THE ADVENTURES
OF TOM SAWYER

A Boy Becomes a Man

Walter Blair

Walter Blair suggests that in *Tom Sawyer* Twain shows his antipathy toward the structure of conventional tales for children by presenting a new concept: a normal history of boyhood and transition to adulthood. He notes that each episode of the novel begins with Tom's boyish action and ends with signs of mature virtue, which receive adult approval. Blair, who co-edited the University of California Press edition of *Huckleberry Finn*, has written widely on American humor and tall tales.

A contemporary critic [of *Tom Sawyer*] said:

> This literary wag has performed some services which entitle him to the gratitude of his generation. He has run the traditional Sunday-school boy through his literary mangle and turned him out washed and ironed into a proper state of collapse. That whining, canting, early-dying, anaemic creature was held up to mischievous lads as worthy of imitation. He poured his religious hypocrisy over every honest pleasure a boy had. He whined his lachrymous warnings on every playground. He vexed their lives. So when Mark grew old enough, he went gunning for him, and lo, wherever his soul may be, the skin of the strumous young pietist is now neatly tacked up to view on the Sunday-school door of to-day as a warning.[1]

That the attack thus suggested may have been responsible in part for the organization of the narrative becomes clear if the story is restated in the way it would have been handled in the literature attacked. The opening chapter of Clemens' novel reveals a character who, in terms of moralizing juvenile literature, has the indubitable earmarks of a Bad Boy. As the story opens, Tom is stealing. Caught in the act, he avoids punishment by deceiving his aunt. He departs to play hookey, returns to stand slothfully by while a slave boy does

---

1. Quoted in Will M. Clemens, *Mark Twain His Life and Work* (Chicago, 1894), p. 126. The writer is identified as "a well-known literary critic," and the passage is drawn from a review. I have been unable, however, to find the original review.

his chores for him, then enters the house to deceive his aunt again. His trickery exposed by his half-brother, Sid, he dashes out of the door shouting threats of revenge. A few minutes later, he is exchanging vainglorious boasts with a stranger whom he hates simply because the stranger is cleanly and neatly dressed. The action of the chapter concludes with Tom pounding the strange boy into submission (for no righteous reason), then chasing him home. "At last," says the author, "the enemy's mother appeared, and called Tom a bad, vicious vulgar child. . . ." If earlier moral writers had had a chance at Tom, they would have been much more eloquent, for within a few pages he has committed many of the enormities against which they had battled for years.

But as the story continues, Bad Boy Tom continues to sin (as these authors would have put it) in a fashion almost unprecedented in the fiction of the time. Up to the last page of chapter X, he piles up enough horrible deeds to spur the average Sunday school author to write pages of admonitions. His actions are of a sort to show that he is—in the language of such an author—thievish, guileful, untruthful, vengeful, vainglorious, selfish, frivolous, self-pitying, dirty, lazy, irreverent, superstitious and cowardly.

What a chance for sermonizing! But Clemens makes nothing of his opportunity: he indicates not the least concern about his hero's mendacity. In fact, his preaching (such as it is) is of a perverse sort. Instead of clucking to show his horror, he writes of Tom's sins with a gusto which earlier authors had reserved for the deeds of Good Boys, and on occasion (as when he tells about the whitewashing trick), he actually commends the youth for his chicanery. A ragged ruffian named Huckleberry Finn who smokes and swears is set up as an ideal figure because

> he did not have to go to school or to church, or call any being master or obey anybody; he could go fishing or swimming when and where he chose, and stay as long as it suited him; nobody forbade him to fight; he could sit up as late as he pleased; . . . . he never had to wash, nor put on clean clothes; he could swear wonderfully. In a word, everything that goes to make life precious, that boy had. So thought every harassed, hampered, respectable boy in St. Petersburg [chap. VI].

On the other hand, the sort of spiteful disdain which had been used to chasten Bad Boys in other books is actually employed here to introduce an indubitable Good Boy. To church on Sunday, says Clemens, last of all came the Model Boy, Willie Mufferson, taking as heedful care of his mother as if she were cut glass. He always brought his mother to church, and was the pride of all the matrons. The boys hated him, he was so good. And besides, he had been "thrown up to them" so much. His white handkerchief was hanging out of his pocket behind, as usual on Sundays—accidentally. Tom had no handkerchief, and he looked upon boys who had, as snobs.

POETIC JUSTICE OUTRAGED

The ending of the book departs as determinedly from the patterns of juvenile fiction. It staggers the imagination to guess the sort of punishment which would have been deigned fitting for such a monster as Tom by fictionists who had felt hanging in adulthood was an appropriate result of youthful truancy. From their standpoint, the author of *Tom Sawyer* must have outraged poetic justice to the point of being hideously immoral. Here were Tom and his companions, who had run away, played truant, and smoked to boot, actually lionized because they returned from Jackson's Island. Here was Tom cheered to the echo because he saved an unjustly accused man, compared with George Washington by Judge Thatcher because he took Becky's punishment, lionized because he saved the girl from the cave.[2] More shocking, here was even the unregenerate Huck dramatically saving the life of the Widow Douglas. And to top it all, these boys were allowed at the end to accumulate a fortune of the size exclusively awarded to only the best of the Alger heroes.

Thus the characterization, the perverse preaching, the unconventional ending of the book, which gave the volume in its day a comic appeal now all but irrecoverable, also, it is possible, did much to mold the form of the narrative. The simplest explanation of the arrangement of happenings in Clemens' book is that it represented a fictional working-out of the author's antipathy to the conventional plot structure of juvenile tales. Here, in other words, is . . . a reversed moralizing narrative.

2. A feminine critic so strongly conditioned by preachy literature that she managed to find a moral, of all places, in *Huckleberry Finn*, in 1887 called attention to outstanding examples of Tom's nobility. "Only a noble and tender heart," she said admiringly, "could have taken the blame upon itself when Becky accidentally tore the teacher's book, and received 'without an outcry the most merciless flogging that even Mr. Dobbins had ever administered,' and 'when he stepped forward to go to his punishment the surprise, the gratitude, the adoration that shone upon him out of poor Becky's eyes seemed to pay enough for a hundred floggings.' The scene in the cave, of the rough boy folding in his arms the lost and weeping little girl, is a beautiful one."—Sarah K. Bolton, *Famous American Authors* (New York, 1887), p. 369.

BECOMING AN ADULT

One effect of this method of telling a story was, of course, to give youthful readers exactly the sort of a series of happenings likely to please them. Here was the story of a character who, in their opinion, was a real boy, a character who, furthermore, time after time, when he was idolized for his achievements, fulfilled the sort of daydreams which had been their own.[3]

A second effect was perhaps even more important. In attacking in other than a burlesque fashion fictional representations of boys who were unreal, Clemens was faced with the problem of depicting, through characterization and plot, boys who were real.[4] What a real boy was was suggested by the very terms of the attack: he was not simply good or bad but a mixture of virtue and mischievousness. And he could play pranks at the same time he was developing qualities which would make him a normal adult.

This concept allowed elements of incongruity which an author might develop humorously. In this view, youngsters of Tom's age were diverting combinations of ignorance and wisdom, deviltry and morality, childhood and adulthood. These incongruities, of course, were useful to Clemens again and again.[5] But the incongruities of boy nature not only had humorous possibilities; they also had potentialities—far beyond those in good-bad-boy books—for plot structures closely linked with developing characters. As a "real" boy grew up, the common sense theory implied, unlike the consistent actions of the static character in goody-goody books, the nature of his actions would change. Not only would they change from year to year but also from month to month. Less and less, he would behave like an irresponsible and ignorant

---

3. Booth Tarkington's shrewd suggestion is that Clemens gave his youthful character "adventures that all boys, in their longing dreams, make believe they have. He made extravagant, dramatic things happen to them; they were pitted against murderers, won their ladyloves, and discovered hidden gold. He made them so real that their very reality is the stimulus of the adult reader's laughter, but he embedded this reality in the romance of a plot as true to the conventional mid-nineteenth century romantic novel-writing as it was to the day-dreams the boy Mark Twain himself had been."—Introduction to Cyril Clemens, *My Cousin Mark Twain* (Emmaus, Pa., 1939). 4. Clemens at least wanted to do this. "Part of my plan," he said in his preface, "has been to try to pleasantly remind adults of how they thought and talked, and what queer enterprises they sometimes engaged in." 5. The famous whitewashing scene, to cite one example, played upon some of these discrepancies: Tom, vainly trying to escape his chore, was the mischievous and ignorant boy. When, later, he got other boys, less canny than he, to do the job for him, he displayed the sort of wisdom—perhaps even of morality—becoming to an adult. "He," said his approving historian, "had discovered a great law of human action, without knowing it—namely, that in order to make a man or boy covet a thing, it is only necessary to make the thing difficult to attain."

savage; more and more he would act like a responsible and intelligent adult.

If *Tom Sawyer* is regarded as a working out in fictional form of this notion of a boy's maturing, the book will reveal, I believe, a structure on the whole quite well adapted to its purpose. My suggestion, in other words, is that Clemens' divergence from the older patterns of juvenile fiction and his concept of the normal history of boyhood led him to a way of characterizing and a patterning of action which showed a boy developing toward manhood.

FOUR LINES OF ACTION

That this was the unifying theme of the story will be indicated, perhaps, by a consideration of the units of narrative, the lines of action, in the novel. There are four of these—the story of Tom and Becky, the story of Tom and Muff Potter, the Jackson's Island episode, and the series of happenings (which might be called the Injun Joe story) leading to the discovery of the treasure. Each one of these is initiated by a characteristic and typically boyish action. The love story begins with Tom's childishly fickle desertion of his fiancée, Amy Lawrence; the Potter narrative with the superstitious trip to the graveyard; the Jackson's Island episode with the adolescent revolt of the boy against Aunt Polly, and Tom's youthful ambition to be a pirate; the Injun Joe story with the juvenile search for buried treasure. Three of these narrative strands, however, are climaxed by a characteristic and mature sort of action, a sort of action, moreover, directly opposed to the initial action. Tom chivalrously takes Becky's punishment and faithfully helps her in the cave; he defies boyish superstition and courageously testifies for Muff Potter; he forgets a childish antipathy and shows mature concern for his aunt's uneasiness about him. The Injun Joe story, though it is the least useful of the four so far as showing Tom's maturing is concerned, by showing Huck conquering fear to rescue the widow, has value as a repetition—with variations—of the motif of the book.

That these actions are regarded by the older folk of St. Petersburg as evidences of mature virtue is suggested in each instance by their reactions. Every subplot in the book eventuates in an expression of adult approval. Sometimes this is private, like Aunt Polly's discovery that Tom has come from the island to tell her of his safety, or like Judge Thatcher's enthusiastic comments upon Tom's chivalry at school. Sometimes it is public, like the adulation lavished on the hero after the trial and after the rescue of Becky, or like the widow's party honoring Huck Finn.

The book contains various episodes extraneous to these lines of action—episodes whose only value in the scheme is variation in the display of the incongruities of boy nature from which the actions arise, but it is notable how much of the novel is concerned with these four threads. Only four of the thirty-five chapters are not in some way concerned with the development of at least one of them. Hence a large share of the book is concerned with actions which show the kind of development suggested.

More important is the fact that, if the novel is regarded as one narrative including the alternately treated lines of action and the episodes as well, as the story progresses, wholly boylike actions become more infrequent while adult actions increase. No such simple and melodramatic a device as a complete reformation is employed: late in the book, Tom is still capable of treasure hunts and fantasies about robber gangs. (Clemens remarked that he "didn't take the chap beyond boyhood.")[6] But actions which are credible late in the story—actions such as Tom's taking Becky's punishment (chap. XX) or testifying for Potter (chap. XXIII)—would, I think, seem improbable early in the book.[7] One of a few slips Clemens makes strengthens this point: in chapter XXIV, Tom tells Huck that when he is rich he is "going to buy a new drum, and sure 'nough sword, and a red necktie and a bull pup, and get married." Mr. Edgar Lee Masters finds this jarring. "Can any boy of that age," he asks, "be imagined talking in this way. . . . ?" It is jarring in chapter XXIV, to be sure, but at any point in the first five chapters of the book, say, it would be highly appropriate.

THE DEVELOPMENT OF CHARACTER

There is perhaps, then, reason for believing that the theme, the main action, and the character portrayal in the novel are one— the developing of Tom's character in a series of crucial situations. Studying the progress of the novel with this in mind, the reader will see, I believe, that though the earlier chapters em-

6. *Letters*, I, 258   7. Two kinds of probability are, I believe, theoretically involved here— one that which represents the intelligent person's general conception of the way a boy matures, the other that which derives from a study of the character of Tom as it is displayed in the book. In this instance, I think, the two kinds of probability coincide.

phasize Tom's mischievousness, and though a Sunday school fictionist would therefore call him a Bad Boy, there are potentialities in these chapters for his later behavior.[8] To put the matter negatively, his motives are never vicious; to put it positively, he has a good heart. In his aunt's words, he

> warn't *bad*, so to say—only misch*ee*vous. Only just giddy, and harum-scarum, you know. He warn't any more responsible than a colt. *He* never meant any harm, and he was the best-hearted boy that ever was [chap. XV].

An appeal to his sympathy, he himself indicates in chapter II, is more efficacious than physical punishment or scolding. "She talks awful," he says of Aunt Polly, "but talk don't hurt—anyways it don't if she don't cry." Inevitably then, when at the end of chapter X, his aunt weeps over him, "this was worse than a thousand whippings." And a chapter later, tender-hearted Tom is ministering to poor Muff Potter as he languishes in jail.

Significant, too, is Tom's acceptance, in times of stress in the early chapters, of the adult code of the particularly godly folk of idyllic St. Petersburg.[9] His feeling that it would be pleasant to die disappears when he remembers that he does not have "a clean Sunday-school record" (chap. VIII), and the howling dog's prophecy of his death brings regret that he has been "playing hookey and doing everything a feller's told *not* to do." "But if I ever get off this time," he promises, "I lay I'll just *waller* in Sunday-schools!" (chap. X). Surrounded by night on Jackson's Island, he inwardly says his prayers, and a little later, his conscience gnaws as he recalls his sins (chap. XIII). He wants to be a soldier, or a plainsman, or a pirate chiefly in order that he may stroll into the drowsy little St. Petersburg church some Sunday morning and bask in the respect of the village (chap. VIII). And his impelling desire for a place of honor in the community is a key to his initiating three of the four lines of action, hence the plot strands are closely linked with his character.

Beginning with the final pages of chapter X, these potentialities for something more mature than inconsiderate

8. If Clemens' book was to be on a level above that of travesty, such potentialities had to be indicated. A rule of literary art which Twain himself formulated in "Fenimore Cooper's literary offenses," in *Literary Essays* (New York, 1899), p. 81, was "that the characters in a tale shall be so clearly defined that the reader can tell beforehand what each will do in a given emergency." Thus his very divergence from the simple motivation of earlier fictional works necessitated more complex characterization than they contained. 9. Kind-hearted Muff Potter, the grave-robbing Dr. Robinson, and the Temperance Tavern keeper who bootlegs are the nearest approach to native sin. Injun Joe and his vague companion from somewhere "up the river" are not of the community. The chief hints of vice Tom picks up anywhere are in the novels he reads.

childhood begin to develop. Tom is touched by his aunt's appeal to his sympathy; his conscience hurts because of his silence about Potter's innocence; he suffers pangs because he
realizes he has sinned in running away; he worries about his
aunt's concern for his safety, and so on. And well in the second half of the book, in a series of chapters—XX, XXIII,
XXIX, XXXII—come those crucial situations in which he
acts more like a grownup than like an irresponsible boy.

GOING OVER TO THE SIDE OF THE ENEMY

There are some indications that Clemens was aware of the
pattern I have suggested. . . . Did he perceive, however, that
deliberate divergence from older patterns had led him to
create a new structure of his own, nearer to the history of
boyhood as he and others conceived it? It is impossible to be
sure, but some facts may have a bearing on the problem.

In Clemens' "Conclusion" to *Tom Sawyer* (the italics are
his) he wrote: "So endeth this chronicle. It being strictly a
history of a *boy*, it must stop here; the story could not go
much further without becoming the history of a *man*." When
in 1875 he wrote Howells asking him to read the manuscript,
Mark Twain asked him particularly to "see if you don't really
decide that I am right in closing with him as a boy."[10] And
writing to Howells, shortly after the critic had read the manuscript, the humorist said he had decided to discard or not
to write what would have been chapter XXXVI, and to add
nothing in its place. "Something told me," he said, "that the
book was done when I got to that point"—presumably, from
the context, the present concluding chapter (XXXV) of the
book.[11]

The concluding passage in this chapter tells how Huck
Finn, tired of civilization, sneaked away from the widow and
started to live again a life free from adult restraints. In chapter VI, it may be recalled, this sort of life had been, in Tom's
opinion, most enviable: "everything that goes to make life
precious, that boy had." So Tom had thought when all adult
curbs had been hateful to him, when grown folk had seemed
to be natural enemies, and their ways unnatural ways. But
now Tom, bent on dragging Huck back to that civilization,

---

10. *Letters*, I, 259 11. Clemens wrote: "As to that last chapter, I think of just leaving it
off and adding nothing in its place. Something told me the book was done when I got
to that point—and so the temptation to put Huck's life into detail, instead of generalizing it in a paragraph was resisted" (*ibid.*, I, 267).

tells the runaway that everybody lives cleanly and according to schedule. "And besides," he urges, "if you'll try this sort of thing just awhile longer you'll come to like it." Craftily, when Huck's chance remark helps Tom "see his opportunity," Tom dangles the bait of the robber gang. But though in chapter XIII Huck in rags was eligible for piratehood and even as late as chapter XXXIII his savagery has not been mentioned as a bar to his joining the robbers, now, to lure the boy back to the Widow's, Tom insists that Huck the Red-handed will have to live with the good woman and be "respectable" if he is to be allowed to join the gang. Something has happened to Tom. He is talking more like an adult than like an unsocial child. He has, it appears, gone over to the side of the enemy.

A Celebration of Innocence

William C. Spengemann

One of the themes of *Tom Sawyer* is Twain's celebration of innocence, especially as a re-creation of his own boyhood, according to William C. Spengemann. But the author's shifting points of view betray his increasing contempt for his hero, who abandons his innocence and voluntarily joins the adult world Twain despises. However, Spengemann writes, at the end of the book Huck Finn hints that he will escape such a fate in the novel that will later be written about him. Spengemann has also written books on American fiction and on autobiography as literature.

In *The Gilded Age* and *Tom Sawyer* Clemens attempts to treat initiation as a fortunate circumstance, but because his sympathies are hopelessly divided, the experiment is unsuccessful in both books. In the former he was urged by his collaborator to turn an innocent into a tragic heroine by having her confront evil, but succeeded only in making her pathetic and sentimental. In the latter, the innocent joyously accepts wealth and adult responsibility, but he is, in the author's eyes, a failure as a man for this very reason. Clemens demonstrates in these two works his growing reluctance to see adulthood as anything but the absence of innocence, a time of senseless constraint and despair, and a state whose dominant emotion is nostalgia for lost youth. . . .

[*Tom Sawyer*] contains three distinct themes, and these stem from three aims which led Clemens to write it. In the first place, *Tom Sawyer* is a revision of "A Boy's Manuscript," which is largely an adult's amused view of childhood. Second, Clemens set out to recreate his own boyhood as he remembered it, to portray innocence with all the attractions which Laura remembers in her death scene. Third, since

Clemens wanted to show that a bad boy could succeed as well as the good boys of pietistic children's fiction, he told a story in which a boy attains wealth and respectability even though he has all the traits which the conventional works condemned. The first of these aims contributes nothing to the second; and the last two work against each other, for Tom's eventual reconciliation with the forces of adult, civilized society—which the satire on the successful good-boy demands—violates Clemens' basic distrust of society, which prompted him to celebrate natural innocence in the first place.

This conflict causes Clemens repeatedly to shift his opinion of his hero. When Tom is a child in an adult's world, he is foolish and earns the reader's tolerant amusement. When he is an innocent, he is sympathetic, an object of admiration and envy. And when he is a candidate for respectability, a burgeoning citizen, a bad boy who is on his way to making good, Clemens treats him with contempt and even hostility.

SHIFTING POINT OF VIEW

These attitudes appear in the novel as three different points of view. When Tom is a foolish boy, a holdover from "A Boy's Manuscript," Clemens poses as an amused adult, who is close to the reader and detached from his hero. When Tom is an innocent, Clemens identifies himself with the boy, attends closely to his unspoken thoughts and emotions, and sees the world through Tom's eyes. And when Tom is in the process of succeeding, Clemens again stands detached from him; but in this case the author is not the amused adult but someone who agrees with Huck Finn in the final chapters.

Clemens' opinions of the book after its completion encourage a search for such internal conflicts. In a letter to Howells, he says that the book is finished and that he will not carry Tom beyond boyhood: "If I went on, now, and took him into manhood, he would be just like all the one-horse men in literature and the reader would conceive a hearty contempt for him."[1] He says elsewhere that the boy would grow up to be "an ordinary liar," and in an interview with [Rudyard] Kipling he remarked, "I had a notion of writing the sequel to *Tom*

1. H.N. Smith and W.M. Gibson, eds., *The Mark Twain–Howells Letters: The Correspondence of Samuel L. Clemens and William D. Howells, 1872–1910*, 2 vols. (Cambridge, Mass.: Belknap Press of Harvard University Press, 1960), p. 91. © Copyright, 1960, by the Mark Twain Company.

Sawyer in two ways. In one I would make him rise to great honor and go to Congress, and in the other I should hang him."[2] Another comment to Howells suggests that the difficulty lies in the narrative mode Clemens used in writing *Tom Sawyer*. He says in the letter quoted above, "I perhaps made a mistake in not writing it in the first person . . . By and by I shall take a boy of twelve and run him through life (in the first person) but not Tom Sawyer—he would not be a good character for it."[3] Apparently Clemens was satisfied with that part of the novel which he related through Tom's eyes but not with those portions which he told as a detached observer. Significantly, the passages which stick most closely to Tom's point of view are those which portray him as an innocent—those which see him without treating him as a childish buffoon or as a reprehensible adult.

HANDLING THE MATTER OF INNOCENCE

The conflicts which account for Tom's changing nature can be illuminated, I believe, by an examination of passages from the novel in which the three points of view are apparent. This analysis can also provide some useful information about Clemens' developing method of handling the matter of innocence; and it can help to explain why he selected Huck as the boy to tell his own story in the sequel to *Tom Sawyer*.

In those portions of the narrative in which the author is most sympathetic to Tom, the boy is a typical innocent. He is an orphan, and although Aunt Polly refers once to her "own dead sister," she never mentions his father or other details of his origin. Tom's main desire is to be free, and he looks at the institutions of St. Petersburg—school, church, family—as "captivity and fetters." His aunt punishes him with "captivity at hard labor," and his first act in the book is to attempt an escape. There is a restraint about "clothes and cleanliness that galled him," and on Jackson's Island he goes naked. Furthermore, the restraint of the town is not entirely of his own imagining, for Clemens says that the strain of memorizing scriptures drove the German boy insane and that a sermon "dealt in limitless fire and brimstone and thinned the predestined elect down to a company so small as to be hardly worth the saving."

2. New York *Herald*, August 17, 1890. Quoted in Svend Peterson, *Mark Twain and the Government* (Caldwell, Idaho: Caxton Printers, Ltd. 1960), p. 37.   3. *The Mark Twain–Howells Letters*, p. 92. © Copyright, 1960, by the Mark Twain Company.

As an innocent, Tom has a good heart. He tells Jim not to mind Aunt Polly's scolding: "She talks awful, but talk don't hurt—anyways it don't if she don't cry." When she weeps over him for his mischief, it is "worse than a thousand whippings" to him. His native compassion has the most room to operate during his escape into the wilderness of Jackson's Island. Returning home, he sees Aunt Polly asleep in her chair, and "his heart [is] full of pity for her." Later he relieves her sorrow about his failure to let her know that he was not dead but only "run off."

Passages which typify Clemens' close personal handling of his hero are those in which Tom contemplates unspoiled nature. As an innocent, his proper domain is the uninhabited countryside; and although the entire setting of the novel provides escape by carrying the reader back to a sinless "canonized epoch," Clemens distinguishes between the innocent woods and fields and the evil town within the larger context. He describes Jackson's Island through Tom's eyes, underscoring the innocent's kinship with nature. As the boy sits basking in "a delicious sense of repose and peace," he watches a measuring worm crawl over him, talks to a ladybug, and touches a tumblebug. A catbird sings to him, and a jay and a squirrel come within his reach unafraid. Similarly, when the innocent is trapped in the town, he looks out of the school window, and Clemens describes both the summer scenery and Tom's longing to be free: "Away off in the flaming sunshine Cardiff Hill lifted its soft green sides through a shimmering veil of heat, tinted with the purple of distance; a few birds floated on lazy wing high in the air; no other living thing was visible but some cows, and they were asleep."

As long as Clemens treats Tom as an innocent, he maintains this idyllic, rustic setting. Like the Innocent Land of *Roughing It* and "Captain Stormfield," and of Laura's memories in *The Gilded Age*, it is dreamy, fanciful, hazy. When the boys run off, Jackson's Island becomes the primeval wood which offers escape from civilized constraint. Their trip there is a momentary denitiation, since they turn their backs on society, casting off their clothes and behaving like savages. Clemens describes their exploring expedition: "They tramped gaily along, over decaying logs, through tangled underbrush, among solemn monarchs of the forest, hung from their crowns to the ground with a drooping regalia of grapevines. Now and then they came upon snug nooks carpeted with grass and jeweled with flowers." This blissful garden is the appropriate setting for the innocent, as is Cardiff Hill, which the author describes as a "Delectable Land," far from the village, "dreamy, reposeful, inviting."

Tom Sawyer is full of magic and the supernatural. Superstition, as Walter Blair remarks [in *Mark Twain and Huck Finn*], is an appropriate element in the boy's story because it was so prevalent in the author's own childhood. Clemens' attention to ghostly atmosphere in all his books about innocence may result from his recollections of his own boyhood. Furthermore, magic in *Tom Sawyer* is confined almost exclusively to the boy's world, and it generally works best away from the village. Huck's remedy for warts requires that the afflicted go into the woods, and Tom's rituals for finding lost marbles and for communing with the doodlebugs are effective on Cardiff Hill. Magic and spectral portents surround the boys' most important adventures: the night in the graveyard, the search for the treasure, and the eventual discovery of gold in MacDougal's Cave.

As an innocent, then, Tom lives in an idyllic world of freedom and wonder; and as an innocent he has stature which transcends his importance as a mischievous backwoods boy. Clemens provides him with virtual symbolic status by attending seriously to his innocent qualities of isolation, good-heartedness, and freedom.

Probably the best example of Tom as a foolish youngster appears in the passage in which the lovesick boy moons over the "Adored Unknown" and lies down beneath her window. This episode is a revised portion of "A Boy's Manuscript"— as are most of the early encounters between Tom and Becky. Clemens' rather patronizing attitude toward Tom in these sections apparently stems from the earlier version. This attitude is evident not only in the boy's ridiculous antics, which separate him from the adult's world and invite the reader's good-natured amusement, but in the author's language as well. Although Clemens attunes his ear to Tom's innermost feelings in this passage he reports these emotions in a language that mocks the boy and encourages the reader to smile knowingly on the absurdly romantic youth. For example, he calls Tom a "poor little sufferer" and a "martyr"; he makes him use a string of hollow clichés to report his "dismal felicity." These sketches of Tom's childishness provide a good beginning for the hero who is to mature, but neither his youth nor his maturity is compatible with his innocence. The former precludes the sublimity of innocence, and the latter denies the basic qualities of that state.

THE SUCCESSFUL BAD BOY

That side of Tom's character which emerges from Clemens' desire to depict the successful bad boy is distinctly not innocent. In the whitewashing episode Tom behaves like an unscrupulous entrepreneur, taking advantage of his fellows for personal gain. After duping Ben Harper, he sits on his barrel, munching his apple and planning "the slaughter of more innocents." In the course of the day he "bankrupts" every boy in the village, and so rises from the position of a "poverty-stricken boy" to that of a capitalist "literally rolling in wealth." His business venture at Sunday school is similarly profitable. At the beginning he tries to learn his lessons "under the double pressure of curiosity and prospective gain." Mary satisfies both when she gives him a knife for his trouble. At church he trades "the wealth he had amassed in selling whitewashing privileges" for tickets on the prize Bible. When he claims the reward, his victims appropriately call him "a wily fraud, a guileful snake in the grass." His speculation appears especially unattractive when we learn that Mary, an unswervingly sympathetic character, acquired two Bibles by "the patient work of two years."

Tom progresses in the book from carelessness to responsibility. Walter Blair says, "Each of several lines of action begins with Tom's behaving in an irresponsible childish fashion and ends with an incident signifying his approach to responsible maturity." The trouble is that with approaching maturity Tom becomes a respectable and accepted figure in St. Petersburg society. Walter Blair illustrates Tom's progress by saying, "At the end, in a conversation with Huck, Tom, although still a boy, is talking very much like an adult." In that dialogue Tom is trying to convince Huck to become respectable, too. Huck complains about the constraint and regularity of the Widow's routine and says that he can't stand it. Tom explains, "Well, everybody does that way, Huck"; and Huck counters, "Tom, it don't make no difference. I ain't everybody." Clemens' sympathies are clearly with Huck in this exchange, for the unregenerate boy is asserting his right to be a free individual while Tom has gone over to the other side; he has sold out his freedom and innocence for accep-

tance and security. Earlier in the book Tom was the bad boy,
but by the end the townspeople treat him as one of themselves. Judge Thatcher has plans for Tom to be "a lawyer or
a great soldier" and to send him to the "National Military
Academy." He has the boy's money out at six percent, giving
him a comfortable income.

HUCK AS THE SYMBOL OF FREEDOM

But while Tom has capitulated, Huck remains true to his innocent desire to be free. He is appalled at Tom's plans to get
married, and swears that he will never let a girl "comb" him.
Again Clemens is on Huck's side in the argument. These
conversations in which Tom argues for convention and
Huck remains skeptical foreshadow the respective characters the two boys will take in *Huckleberry Finn.*

There is evidence throughout the novel of the author's increasing interest in Huck; he must have had this boy in mind
when he told Howells that he wanted to tell a boy's story in
the first person. Huck's main attraction for Clemens, it
seems, is his refusal to be initiated, for although he accepts
his half of the money and agrees to return to the Widow's
(presumably for the sake of a tidy ending), he begins his
own story by giving up the money and leaving the Widow
again. He has been the symbol of freedom since the first of
Tom Sawyer. He has "everything that goes to make life precious," in the opinion of "every harassed, hampered, respectable boy in St. Petersburg." He is democratic, for he eats
with the Negroes, although civilized convention frowns on
such fraternizing.

Clemens seems to have recognized by this time, at least
vaguely, that in order to keep his innocent from being sul-
lied by the comments of the adult narrator, he would have to
let him tell his own story. At the end of the novel, the author
is obviously disappointed with Tom, whom he has forced
into conformity and respectability; but Huck already has
many of the attractions which would make Clemens select
him as the hero of the sequel. *Tom Sawyer* is the story of an
initiation into society; *Huckleberry Finn* would take up the
escape theme again. However appealing the former book
may be to the reader, it was unsatisfactory to Clemens, for it
pointed toward the same fate that Laura had suffered, and it
ends with Tom's blind acceptance of the adult responsibility
which the author had tried to throw off by writing it.

Tom Sawyer, with its nostalgic setting, then, seems to be Clemens' objectification of Laura's lost world of innocence. But the serpent creeps into St. Petersburg just as it did into Hawkeye, and once again it comes in the form of money. Because he wanted to make Tom a bad boy who emerges accepted and respectable from his irresponsible childhood, he destroyed his hero's innocence. Clemens' experiments in *The Gilded Age* and *Tom Sawyer*, unsuccessful as they are in certain respects, were not altogether fruitless, however, for out of the two books he salvaged a hero, a point of view, and a setting, which would provide a basis for *Huckleberry Finn*.

Games of Death

Harold Aspiz

Death and resurrection, which are major elements in
Tom Sawyer, provide a dark contrast that sets off
Twain's sweet memories of childhood, writes Harold
Aspiz. Aspiz ties these youthful reveries to the grim
horror of murder, noting Twain's repetition of death
and resurrection themes until the final "jolly game of
death" as the town celebrates the demise of Injun Joe.
Besides essays on various literary figures, Aspiz has
also written a book on American poet and Twain contemporary Walt Whitman.

The Adventures of Tom Sawyer is constructed on a loose
framework whose major elements include games of death
and games of resurrection. (Both meanings of resurrection
apply here: resurrection as grave robbing and resurrection
as return to life from apparent death.) Indeed, the world of
Tom Sawyer—Mark Twain's remembered and reinvented
world of childhood—appears to be piquant and sweet largely
because it is seen in chiaroscuro—a bright world set off by
the shadowy terrors of danger, death and conformity. Young
Tom—and obliquely through him the self-recreated young
Sam Clemens—seems to exist on the manic edge beyond
which lurks the menace of destruction and the unknown.
Tom is a manchild continually living at risk in this child's
world where the adults often appear to be custom-bound
conformists with whom Tom has no quarrel provided they
do not threaten him or interfere too much with the hijinks
he shares with his juvenile companions. Inevitably, however, he is nourished by the values of this adult world.

Young Tom is no budding John Keats, but his romantic
soul is titillated by the bittersweet thought of his own death.
Twain delightfully captures those emotional moments in a
child's life when the thought of one's own demise seems to
loom like a dark cloud—moments upon which the adult self

Excerpted from "Tom Sawyer's Game of Death," by Harold Aspiz, *Studies in the Novel*,
vol. 27, no. 2 (Summer 1995), pp. 141–153. Reprinted by permission of the University
of North Texas.

may look back in bemused fascination. And true romantic that he is, Tom relishes these moments. On the Saturday evening following his triumphant ploy in persuading his young friends to whitewash his Aunt Polly's fence and his subsequent feeling "that it was not such a hollow world, after all" he becomes depressed and sulky because his aunt has wrongfully blamed him rather than his pampered kid brother Sid for breaking a cookie jar. Recognizing her look of tearful contrition when she realizes her error, Tom bolsters his male ego by playing a consoling and satisfying game of death, imagining that he is "lying sick unto death" and not speaking a word to his grieving and repentant aunt. "Ah, how would she feel then?" he fantasizes. To vary the fantasy, he also imagines that he has been brought home after he has drowned in the river, "a poor little sufferer, whose griefs were at an end," and imagines that his grief-stricken aunt lies ill, broken with anguish over her mistreatment of him. So satisfying is this game of nursing his self-mourning that rather than risking its disruption by cheerful thoughts he runs off . . . to be alone with his tremors of mortality. This "agony of pleasurable" suffering is augmented when he imagines that Becky Thatcher (the pretty classmate on whom he has developed a crush) is grieving for him.

But the outside world proves less satisfying than his private fantasies. Tom's euphoria of pleasurable grief is dispelled when, standing under the window of his "adored Unknown," he is doused by a "deluge of water" thrown from the beloved's second story window by the Thatcher housemaid. On the blue Monday following an exciting weekend, and in a ruse to ditch school, Tom again pretends to be dying, upsetting his brother Sid and his Aunt Polly, but he backs off when the old lady threatens to pull one of his loose teeth. Later, surreptitiously playing with a tick at school, he taunts his buddy Joe Harper with the prospect of his own death: "He's my tick and I'll do what I blame please with him, or die." Still later that day, disappointed over his estrangement with Becky Thatcher, he again reverts to the game of imagining himself dead, so that she will be sorry for cruelly spurning him: "Ah, if he could only die, *temporarily*," he is supposed to have thought, thus sounding the keynote for the sort of resurrection game that the author will twice develop and dramatize in the course of the novel to form its most exciting episodes and which he, Twain, will one day introduce into his autobiography, imagining himself enjoying a post mortem tête-a-tête with his future readers long after his own death.

At midnight of that same Monday—to the ominous sounds of a cricket and a deathwatch beetle—Tom sneaks out of the house and goes with Huck Finn to the decaying Baptist graveyard. Frightened to be among the spirits of the dead, they watch in terror as three would-be resurrectionists—Dr. Robinson, Injun Joe, and Muff Potter (respectively a young physician, an arch-villain, and a slow-witted drunkard)—prepare to snatch the body of Horse Williams from its grave. In the darkness, Injun Joe picks a quarrel with Dr. Robinson and murders him, then puts the blame on Muff Potter. Thus the game of death that had been enjoyable as long as Tom could invent his own scenario with himself as the imaginary tragic hero turns horrifying and grim when objectified in the "real" world. And Tom's sense of guilt for hiding the fact that Muff Potter is innocent of Dr. Robinson's death, suppressed because of his fear of Injun Joe, almost devours him during the following weeks as he internalizes what he has witnessed. By way of contrast, his schoolmates, playing a pleasant childhood game of death, hold mock "inquests on dead cats.". . .

MAJOR STRUCTURAL DEVICES

As Mark Twain fumbled for a method to organize and develop the novel, he must have realized the potential of games of death as major structural devices. Indeed, the two climactic episodes of the remainder of the novel involve Tom in games of resurrection—the first one played out as sentimental and idyllic comedy, the second as terror-filled melodrama. As Frank Baldanza has pointed out, "the situation of being thought dead" is an "organizational device" in both *The Adventures of Tom Sawyer* and *The Adventures of Huckleberry Finn.*[1] The first of these resurrection game episodes is the idyll of Jackson's Island, where three boys—Tom, Huck Finn, and Joe Harper—have secretly escaped from the adult world to the carefree place where, for a while, time stands still and adults seem powerless to interfere. Seated by the campfire on the deserted island, which to their young minds is an earthly paradise, Tom wonders, "What would

1. Frank Baldanza, *Mark Twain: An Introduction and Interpretation* (New York: Holt, Rinehart, and Winston, 1961), p. 109

the boys say if they could see us?" To which Joe Harper's re-
ply suggests that the thought of death is never far away:
"Say? Well, they'd just die to be here." Earthly bliss, it would
appear, is only understandable against a background of
death—a concept that would pervade Mark Twain's later
writings. And when the boys observe the boat that is searching the river for their presumably dead bodies, they relish
the idea of being thought dead and grieved for by their families and friends. Thus is acted out a much grander version
of the game that Tom had played in his moments of moping
and mock-grief for his "dead" self. As Mark Twain phrases
the feeling:

> They felt like heroes in an instant. Here was a gorgeous tri-
> umph; they were missed; they were mourned; hearts were
> breaking on their account; tears were being shed; accusing
> memories of unkindnesses to these poor lost lads were rising
> up, and unavailing regrets and remorse were being indulged;
> and best of all, the departed were the talk of the whole town,
> and the envy of all the boys, as far as this dazzling notoriety
> was concerned.

Twain's series of breathless independent clauses catches the
sheer excitement of this game of death played in the se-
questered, if ephemeral, paradise of Jackson's Island.

Eventually tiring of being away from the adult world and
stricken by a conscience that was formed by that same adult
world, Tom sneaks back home at night, hides beneath a bed,
and has the perverse pleasure of hearing his Aunt Polly, his
cousin Mary, Joe Harper's mother, and even his pesky kid
brother Sid linger over his merits and mourn his supposedly
dead self. Tom, too, is silently bathed in tears when he hears
his aunt praying for him. As evidence of his presence there,
after leaving his hiding place under the bed, he kisses the
lips of his sleeping aunt. And to cap off this exhilarating
phase of this game of death, he returns to the island in time
for breakfast! Apparently on Saturday, the fifth day of the
Jackson's Island idyll (and in rather cavalier shifting of the
novel's point of view), we see Tom's little inamorata Becky
Thatcher grieve and cry over the apparent loss of her young
hero. And village folk young and old ascribe to Tom and his
companions the sort of virtues that one might expect to hear
in a eulogy. But Tom, in his own right, is an incomparable
showman. Like P.T. Barnum, whose work Mark Twain admired, and like Mark Twain's later fictional heroes Hank
Morgan and Young Satan, who combined the spectacles of

their own resurrection with dazzling and fiery showmanship, Tom cannot resist climaxing this game of death with
the spectacle of his own resurrection.

Thus, on the last day of this game of death, on Sunday, in
the village church nearly hushed in funereal gloom and despair, with Tom's and Joe's families dressed in mourning,
and the church packed with mourners, the game reaches its
triumphant climax. Following a stirring hymn the minister,
taking as his text "I am the Resurrection and the Life,"
preaches a moving sermon glorifying the "lost" boys. As the
"transfixed" minister looks upward to the church balcony
he sees the three boys who have stealthily entered the
church and "hid in the unused gallery listening to their own
funeral sermon!" Then in a magnificent outburst of theatricality, the general ecstatic rejoicing over the resurrection of
these presumably lost children becomes a vast community
drama as the entire congregation sings "Praise God from
whom all blessings flow." At this point Mark Twain may
have been taunting his readers. Indeed, unless he had chosen to commit brazen sacrilege by setting the scene on
Easter Sunday, he has carried this resurrection game about
as far as he could without overtly mocking the Christian
doctrine of resurrection. The episode is filled with tension,
sentimentality, and suggestiveness.

But we must not forget that the game is Tom's game. For
our budding young Barnum, "this was the proudest moment
of his life." And using one of his favorite words, Mark Twain
acknowledges that the adults of the town were "sold"—
duped, deceived, made to look "almost . . . ridiculous" by this
mock-resurrection with its flaunted irreverence toward
Christian religious views and village decorum. (The community might have felt a momentary twinge of shame or
outrage or may have been tempted to question its value system, but the thrill of hearing the congregation sing "Old
Hundred" outweighed any impulse to self-analysis.) The
town exists largely as a setting for Tom's adventures, and in
his eyes the wave of adulation among the townsfolk and
children crested until "the very summit of glory was
reached"—or almost reached as Becky, ignoring him, cast a
faint shadow of death over him: "it maddened him to see, as
he thought he saw, that Becky Thatcher never once suspected that he was in the land of the living." Nevertheless,
Tom thought, "he would live for glory." "This long episode,"

says Everett Emerson, "ends with Tom's pleasure at what many have wished for and few achieved—a triumphant return to his own funeral." [2] But soon the St. Petersburg adults are disabused, the escapade is forgotten, and the game is over. It was, after all, a glorious capstone to all those little private games in which Tom wished himself dead but still able to hang around to relish the grief and mourning of his loved ones. And although the reader might expect this resurrection to linger in Tom's—and Mark Twain's—mind, nevertheless, after a chapter or so, the author and his hero seem to forget about it and it is not mentioned again as they move on to other episodes. . . .

A DOUBLE PLOT

Because *The Adventures of Tom Sawyer* was composed in a desultory and episodic manner, Twain follows the Jackson's Island episode with lesser happenings. The murder in the graveyard surfaces again, and Tom and Huck are filled with suppressed terror of the murderous Injun Joe and compassion for the falsely accused Muff Potter. The suppressed painful and "dreadful secret of the murder was a chronic misery" to Tom, explains Mark Twain. But Tom once again emerges as "a glittering hero" when he testifies in court about the murder in the graveyard. Later, in a seeming variant of the grave robbery motif, Tom and Huck dig for buried treasure near a haunted house, wherein Injun Joe comes close to discovering and killing them. Perhaps the most important element in this frightening episode is Huck's emergence as a strong colloquial character, thus enabling Mark Twain, for the first time in his fiction-writing career, to develop a double (simultaneous) plot with both suspenseful elements centered on death games. Concurrent with Tom's and Becky's confrontation with death in McDougal's Cave, Huck has his own heroic adventure.

Injun Joe, nursing a deep-seated sense of vengeance against the Widow Douglas (her late husband Judge Douglas had ordered him horsewhipped and jailed as a vagabond) plans to deform the widow. In this novel (unlike *The Adventures of Huckleberry Finn*) the widow is still a handsome woman. Joe plans to "go for her looks," to "slit her nostrils" and "notch her ears like a sow's," then "tie her to the bed. If

2. Everett Emerson, *The Authentic Mark Twain: A Literary Biography of Samuel L. Clemens* (Philadelphia: Univ. of Pennsylvania Press, 1984), p. 82

she bleeds to death, is that my fault?" Mark Twain is generally circumspect in treating the deaths and mutilations of females. They may be beaten, they may die of hunger, disease, or immolation, but they are not sexually violated. However, there can be little doubt that Injun Joe's planned mutilation of the Widow Douglas has undertones of deadly rape, for he plans to violate and deform two of her bodily orifices, her nose and her ears, then watch her bleed to death in her bedroom. When Joe details his planned maiming of the widow, his accomplice cries out, "My God, that's—"; the reader may supply the rest. Overt rape, of course, was hardly suitable stuff for a nineteenth-century boy's book, but it can be interpreted as a significant element in the novel's thematic development. Like the violation of Horse Williams's grave, Injun Joe's planned rape-like assault on the kindly and charitable Widow Douglas is a symbolic violation of the innocent world of St. Petersburg. By thwarting the assault, the arch-innocent Huck Finn rescues the widow from death and ignominy and preserves the town's honor. Like the "resurrection" from Jackson's Island, Huck's rescue of the widow apparently occurs on a Sunday morning.

Chronologically overlapping Huck's adventure are Tom's and Becky's adventures in McDougal's Cave and their eventual escape—an episode possibly inspired by an 1873 news story about some children lost in the Hannibal cave. If the boys' return from Jackson's Island is resurrection as comic spectacle, the episode of the cave—the book's climactic adventure—is resurrection as suspenseful melodrama. The young couple, after being separated from their picnic party, become lost in the cave's vast and trackless caverns, exhaust their candles, and apparently spend three days and nights— Saturday through Monday—in total darkness. The children's descent into the cave becomes a descent into the nether world of sheer terror and the shadow of death. In one of the most romantic passages in all of Mark Twain's fiction, Tom and Becky wander into the uncharted interior of the cave and draw close in their innocent attachment—an episode that would later have its counterpart in Mark Twain's affectionate sketches of Adam and Eve, those idealized versions of Sam and Livy Clemens. But the cave episode involves no fall from Paradise: only a resurrection from the cave and from what the St. Petersburg folk fear to be the deaths of the young pair.

As the children descend among the galleries of "fantastic pillars" of stalactites and stalagmites, they become lost, disoriented, and disheartened. So frenzied is Becky's weeping "that Tom was appalled with the idea that she might die, or lose her reason." In despair, Becky dozes off into a happy dream, but her waking laugh is "stricken dead upon her lips." Her strong premonition of death is conveyed in the conventional terms of sentimental romance: "I've seen such a beautiful country in my dream. I reckon we are going there." Then, in a ritual that is ambiguously connubial or funereal, the pair wander until they find a spring of water—a token of holiness. There in the timeless world of darkness (although the pair speculate that it may be Sunday—"Sabbath morning"—in the outside world), Tom unwraps a bit of "wedding-cake" that Becky had saved from the children's picnic. As Mark Twain unfolds this sentimental/romantic game of death, he has Becky remark: "I saved it from the picnic for us to dream on, Tom, the way grown-up people do with wedding cake—but it'll be our—." There by the underground spring, without hope of rescue, the young pair await their deaths. They watch fascinated as their brief candle— the last "bit of candle"—melts in its niche in the rock and leaves them in total darkness; so that, metaphorically at least, they have carried out their funeral services and have died. But Mark Twain never intended to pursue the quintessential romantic theme of the deaths of children to its tragic conclusion; the book is, after all, a comedy, and soon Tom, although "sick with the bodings of coming doom," is busily exploring the cave again, looking for an exit. And on the third day, he perceives a "speck" of daylight and is able to save himself and Becky.

THE JOLLY GAME OF DEATH

Apparently Mark Twain was careful not to stage Tom's and Becky's "resurrection" on a Sunday. But when the two children return home the church bells peal and the "frantic half-clad" cheering and joyous townspeople fill the town's main street to surround and acclaim the young pair. In his second adventure of return from the dead, Tom is again a hero basking in the adulation he receives and embroidering his tale of derring-do to admiring listeners. And to top off Tom's triumph, he and Huck become rich and Judge Thatcher, bestowing the mantle of bourgeois respectability on him, predicts that one day Tom may become a lawyer or a soldier—a conforming member of the established society. So that what began as a descent into the dark world of terror and death ends as a joyous game; and the elevation to the bourgeoisie that young Sam Clemens had fancied for himself is here bestowed on young Tom.

And by way of eerie counterpoint to Tom's death game, the body of Injun Joe, whom Tom had glimpsed very much alive in the cave near the buried treasure, so close that Joe could have stabbed him (he had kept the terrible secret from Becky), is later discovered by some townsfolk near the mouth of the cave. Joe had died of thirst and starvation. Throughout the novel Joe is portrayed as a cartoon-like villain whose shadow hovers over Tom to cast the thrill of terror over all his joyous game play. But Mark Twain appears to have been uncomfortable with this last bit of melodrama concerning Joe's demise, and he embellishes Joe's death with some purple prose more appropriate to the lecture circuit and with a misplaced sexist sermonette on the soft-hearted "sappy women" who dabble in politics and show sympathy for rascals like Joe. But soon after these awkward digressions the jolly game of death is resumed as the whole town celebrates Joe's death, joining in a chorus of jubilation and fun that may suggest a streak of sadism beneath their apparent respectability.

So end the games of death in *The Adventures of Tom Sawyer*. Never again in Mark Twain's major writings will death games be played with such *élan*, joy, and light-heartedness. . . . But *The Adventures of Tom Sawyer* in its innocence and joy reflects a happy Mark Twain and his idealized dream world of youth in which the games of death—despite some lurking shadows—may still be played as an innocent form of pure adventure. As such, it is a major triumph.

Childhood Innocence Can Transform the Harsh Adult World

James L. Johnson

In Tom Sawyer's world, violent reality can be touched and transformed by a child's innocence, writes James L. Johnson. In the novel, which balances the idyllic world of children with the harsh world of reality, all the brutality comes from adults. This sharp dichotomy reflected Twain's dissatisfaction with the adult world, according to Johnson—a dissatisfaction so great that he had to give credence to the charmed world of children. Johnson's book, *Mark Twain and the Limits of Power*, is a study proposing that Twain's writings are dependent on a Free Self, which he defines as a romantic extension of the ideals of Ralph Waldo Emerson.

Sometime in 1897, while he was in Switzerland, Twain rummaged his memory for details of his boyhood home. His jottings, to which he gave the title "Villagers of 1840–3," record details of the lives of Hannibal residents, and Walter Blair's research has verified most of the biographical information Twain set down. While Twain changed some of the villagers' names, and while some of the events are to a greater or lesser degree invented, Blair cites the fragment as evidence of Twain's "enduring power of recall."[1] The curious thing about the fragment, however, is not so much Twain's accuracy, but the contradiction it evidences between the details he remembered and the generalizations he came to—or felt impelled to include about Hannibal and its populace.

1. Walter Blair, ed., *Mark Twain's Hannibal, Huck and Tom* (Berkeley: Univ. of California Press, 1969), 24. Cited hereafter as *MT's Hannibal*. Bernard DeVoto also briefly discusses the "Villagers" fragment in *Mark Twain at Work* (Cambridge, MA: Harvard Univ. Press, 1942), 15–16, as does Albert Stone in *The Innocent Eye: Childhood in Mark Twain's Imagination* (New Haven: Yale Univ. Press, 1961), 74, both in relation to Twain's prudishness.

The fragment in its manuscript form covers some thirty-four pages (a dozen in its published form), and in that space are recorded nearly twenty instances of prostitution and illicit sex, unnatural deaths (including murder and suspected murder), brutal assaults, and grotesque cases of physical affliction and mental derangement. Of the Ratcliffe family, for example, Twain notes that one son

> had to be locked into a small house in corner of the yard—and chained. Fed through a hole. Would not wear clothes, winter or summer. Could not have a fire. Religious mania. Believed his left hand had committed a mortal sin and must be sacrificed. Got hold of a hatchet, nobody knows how, and chopped it off. Escaped and chased his mother all over the house with a carving knife. (*MT's Hannibal*, 37–38)

Of Sam Bowen, one of Twain's childhood friends, this entry:

> Pilot. Slept with the rich baker's daughter, telling the adoptive parents they were married. The baker died and left all his wealth to "Mr. and Mrs. S. Bowen." They rushed off to a Carondolet magistrate, got married, and bribed him to ante-date the marriage. Heirs from Germany proved the fraud and took the wealth. Sam no account and a pauper. Neglected his wife; she took up with another man. Sam a drinker. Dropped pretty low. Died of yellow fever and whiskey. . . . (*MT's Hannibal*, 32)

The Blankenship daughters were charged with prostitution; a "Hanged Nigger" confessed to the rape and murder of a girl of thirteen, and to the rape of "many . . . white married women who kept it quiet partly from fear of him and partly to escape the scandal"; Ed and Dick Hyde were "tough and dissipated. Ed held his uncle down while Dick tried to kill him with a pistol which refused fire" (*MT's Hannibal*, 31, 369).

And so on. The details accumulate to portray a village with more than its share of depravity, dissipation, and brutality. But in the midst of these reminiscences, Twain could describe quite another village, one in which purity and prudence were watchwords:

> *Chastity:* There was the utmost liberty among young people—but no young girl was ever insulted, or seduced, or even scandalously gossiped about. Such things were not even dreamed of in that society, much less spoken of and referred to as possibilities.

> Two or three times, in the lapse of years, married women were whispered about, but never an unmarried one. (*MT's Hannibal*, 35)

And, apparently ignoring his own entry on Sam Bowen, Twain contrasts the crassness of the nineties with the more spiritual Hannibal of his youth, where among the young folk

> To get rich was no one's ambition—it was not in any young person's thoughts. The heroes of these young people—even the pirates—were moved by lofty impulses: they waded in blood . . . to rescue the helpless, not to make money; they spent their blood and made their self-sacrifices for "Honor's" sake, not to capture a giant fortune; they married for love, not for money or position. It was an intensely sentimental age, but it took no sordid form. (*MT's Hannibal*, 35)

"Villagers of 1840–3" was not written for publication. While the bulk of it reflects fact, it is still a combination of accurate memories and working notes for possible stories (*MT's Hannibal*, 26). There was no need for consistency in what Twain set down, but neither was there any need to distort the picture of Hannibal (referred to in the piece as "St P") into something that never was. Exactly why he did so is probably not ascertainable, but the wild contrast bespeaks a conflict in Twain that appears in most of his major works: a commitment to portraying both a gentle and innocently idyllic world that is patently subjective and imagined, and a world of grotesque harshness that, if not more "real," is at least reflective of a very different order of experience, one much more consonant with actuality. It is this conflict that Richard Chase has in mind when he describes Twain's fictional province as "not the novel proper, but the borderland between novel and romance."[2] It is a conflict between experience as we would wish it to be, and experience as we wish it were not, and Twain was never very successful at drawing a clear distinction between the two—not in his fiction, and to some degree, not in his own thinking. When he took pen in hand, Twain was often given to portraying both worlds. Like a metal rod suspended between two magnets, his imagination swayed now in one direction, now in the other. In somewhat the same way as Emerson with his "parallel lines that never meet," he was plagued with the problem of doing justice to both.

BALANCING TWO ORDERS OF EXPERIENCE

In trying to keep the two orders of experience properly balanced, Twain associated them with two stages of life. In the "Villagers" fragment, one notices that while the brutalities

2. Richard Chase, *The American Novel and Its Tradition* (Garden City, N.Y.: Doubleday, 1957), 156

are ascribed to adults, the idyllic generalizations pertain to children. There are only two passing references in the fragment that ascribe unsavory activities to the children of Hannibal. In one, Twain's childhood sweetheart, Laura Hawkins, "fell out of her chair and Jenny [Brady] made that vicious remark." (The remark itself is not recorded.) In another, one Roberta Jones "scared old Miss - - - - - into the insane asylum with a skull and a doughface" (*MT's Hannibal*, 30, 32). If the "vicious remark" was intentional, the scare trick was performed in fun, and its tragic results were not anticipated. Roberta Jones precipitated tragedy, but she is not held morally accountable.

In the light of the later "Villagers" fragment it is somewhat surprising to see Twain calling Hannibal "this tranquil refuge of my childhood" in *Life on the Mississippi*[3] (*Writings* IX 429). But clearly he was much given to seeing childhood as a "refuge" from the darker problems he associated with adulthood, and in some moods he could very nearly convince himself, or part of himself, that the idyllic world of childhood he imagined was more "real" than—and certainly preferable to— the adult world he actually inhabited. In his account of visiting Hannibal in *Life on the Mississippi*, he tells of climbing Holliday's Hill to get a "comprehensive view" of the village. With the village spread below him, he sees "the town as it was, not as it is": "The things about me and before me made me feel like a boy again—convinced me that I was a boy again, and that I had simply been dreaming an unusually long dream . . ." (*Writings* IX 428–29). The wistful entry into a Hannibal Arcadia is described in metaphors of life and death, freedom and captivity: "I stepped ashore with the feeling of one returned out of a dead-and-gone generation. I had a sort of realizing sense of what the Bastille prisoners must have felt when they used to come out and look upon Paris after years of captivity" (*Writings* IX 428).

The association of childhood with freedom, innocence, and life, and of adulthood with imprisonment, corruption, and death, were to become implicit considerations in Twain's thinking and works. In his mind adulthood carried unacceptable burdens and limitations. The adult was both a victim of and usually a spokesman for a society whose standards were hypocritical and whose workings were base,

3. Mark Twain, *The Writings of Mark Twain* (hereafter cited as *Writings*), 25 vols. (New York: Harper, 1907–18), IX 429

destructive, and cruel. Most of Twain's satiric bent was to be devoted to exposing the falsity and brutality of a society operated by adults.

THE POWER OF THE CHILD'S IMAGINATION

The child, however, lived for Twain in what Kenneth Lynn describes as a "magic circle," [4] a charmed world in which adult hypocrisy and cruelty were largely foreign elements. The child, to Twain's mind, was untainted by base motives of personal gain at the expense of others; he acted spontaneously rather than by craft or guile; he was by nature benevolent; and—a point in which Twain took a special delight—his imagination was incredibly fertile, active, and unfettered. As yet unassimilated into a structured community, the child had no fixed social identity. He was free to adopt any "self" he cared to imagine.

This last characteristic of the child might have remained for Twain no more than a fanciful delight with which to adorn stories for boys and girls. In *The Adventures of Tom Sawyer*, in fact, the narrator's tone is often that of a condescending but indulgent adult chuckling over the extravagant imaginings of a little boy. [5] But it became for Twain, even in *Tom Sawyer*, something more important. It touched on that notion that some part of Twain was willing to take more seriously—the notion that the imagination might be potent enough to clothe itself in reality, that dreams, as with Napoleon, might one day sire a very tangible throne. The charmed circle of the child's world, then, accrued another dimension: the child was not only free and naturally benevolent and innocent; he was also able to touch the real world with his innocent imagination, and to transform it from something resistant and base to something pliable and enjoyable. Unlike the adult, who had to accommodate himself to a world fixed in its outlines and circumstances, it was the child's privilege to arrange the world to satisfy himself.

The distinction Twain made between the worlds of children and adults might well remind one of Emerson's assertion that "old age seems the only disease . . . fever, intemperance, insanity, stupidity and crime; they are all forms of

---

4. Kenneth Lynn, *Mark Twain and Southwestern Humor* (Westport, Conn.: Greenwood Press, 1960), 187 5. James Cox makes a similar point in *Mark Twain: The Fate of Humor* (Princeton: Princeton Univ. Press, 1966), 136, when he says that Tom's play is a "drama [in] which the juvenile reader can believe and the adult reader can indulge with a mixture of nostalgia and gentle irony."

old age."[6] Twain could go ashore at Hannibal and be "convinced . . . that I was a boy again." For a moment it was an escape from time, a Lazarus-like rise from the dead, and he could half believe in that moment that the pressures and disillusionments of his own adulthood could fall away, or at least be reduced from the status of "reality" to that of "dream."

Twain was a complicated man, of course, and any description of his thinking is likely to fall prey to oversimplification. Yet it is necessary to make this claim, at least: so great was his dissatisfaction with the real world that he found it almost *necessary* to give credence to the charmed world of children. This is not to say that he was incapable of distinguishing the real from the imagined. In 1876 he could write to Will Bowen, his best boyhood friend and brother of Sam Bowen, telling him to stop dwelling on the sentimental never-never land of childhood, and denying that the past held anything "worth pickling for present or future use."[7] Nevertheless, both his fiction and his biography testify to a commitment to the charmed circle which was more emotional than logical, and which was largely removed from the clearer sight of a more common, if more prosaic, sense. . . .

INNOCENCE VS. TRUTH

Twain's emotional commitment to the charmed circle of childhood is important. If the adult world was not worth believing in, surely the charmed world was worthy of allegiance. His belief in it was in a way a kind of stopgap to despair; it was a much happier, much kinder, much more satisfactory world. Nevertheless, his devotion to it was destined to become adulterated as he began to paint it in words. For if he was committed to the innocent world of children, he was also, as a novelist, committed to the truth of what it was to be a human being. And as he wrote, he was to discover two problems that tended to undercut his faith in the charmed circle. The first was the fact that, in real life, children inevitably grow up. The same Sam Bowen who once cavorted on Holliday's Hill eventually slept with the rich baker's daughter, perpetrated fraud, and died of yellow fever and whiskey. Experience seemed to lead in one direction:

6. Ralph Waldo Emerson, *The Complete Works of Ralph Waldo Emerson*, ed. Edward Waldo Emerson (Boston: Houghton Mifflin, 1903), II 319 7. Quoted by Dixon Wecter in "Mark Twain," in *The Literary History of the United States*, ed. Robert E. Spiller, et al., 3 vols., 4th rev. ed. (New York: Macmillan, 1953), 929

not out of the Bastille and back to Hannibal, but the other way about, from Hannibal to the Bastille, from freedom to limitation, from potential to disability.

This was a portion of experience that Twain could not accept gracefully, and he had real difficulty portraying it in his fiction. . . . Though he told Howells that he wanted to write a story in which a boy would be carried to adulthood,[8] he could never successfully accomplish it. When it came to the point, something in his deepest imagination rebelled.

The second problem that confronted Twain was more serious. . . . It was all very well for him to contemplate the purity of the empowered child in generalizations. But writing novels required that the generalizations be filled out with details, that the hero become engaged with others, that he respond to the world as well as provoke responses in others. Above all, the hero had to act in a world that the reader could recognize as one roughly equivalent to his own. As Twain placed his empowered figure in such a world, he began to see something troublesome: a mean and destructive egoism that was not at all consonant with what he thought he remembered about children.

Kenneth Lynn sees Twain's early travel books as showing "a lonely American backtrailing in time toward that magic circle" of Hannibal and the child world. "In *The Adventures of Tom Sawyer*, the long voyage is over; Twain's persona is now a boy in Paradise."[9] The world of *Tom Sawyer* is in many ways a Paradise, but only because Twain went to considerable lengths to keep it so, by exorcising from it anything that smacked too strongly of a real world.

8. Frederick Anderson, William M. Gibson, Henry Nash Smith, eds., *Selected Mark Twain–Howells Letters*, 1872–1910 (Cambridge: Belknap Press of Harvard Univ. Press, 1967), 49 9. Lynn, 187

Tension over the Changing American Culture

Peter Messent

Tom Sawyer is often said to glorify childhood in a simpler time, notes Peter Messent. However, he writes, a closer reading of the novel reveals tensions over the changes in America's social and economic order during the last decades of the nineteenth century, the Gilded Age. In keeping with the new social order, Messent says, Tom is part boy, part con man. Messent has written books on Hemingway and on the American novel, and edited collections of essays on the American crime novel and literature of the occult.

It seems, in retrospect, no coincidence that *The Adventures of Tom Sawyer* was published in 1876, the year the United States celebrated the centennial of its nationhood. For the book 'lays claim to being America's most popular novel', and its title character has the status of a 'national icon'[1]—pictured (along with whitewashed fence) on bicentennial stamps, recalled in Disneyland at Tom Sawyer's Island,[2] the repeated subject of films, musicals and other representations. If Tom Sawyer occupies 'the perfect place . . . in our national literature and consciousness',[3] the boy cannot be divorced from his background. For Twain's book has come to stand for a wider 'glorification of life in small-town America',[4] an expression of longing for an earlier time and

1. Lee Clark Mitchell, 'Introduction' to *The Adventures of Tom Sawyer* (Oxford: Oxford University Press, World's Classics, 1993) p. x. This is one of the best recent essays on the novel. 2. Described by Gregg Camfield as 'Like the entire park, . . . [offering] a self-contained haven of adventure, where fantasies of piracy and treasure hunting, of endless summertime and endless youth, are colored with enough that is frightful to make them interesting, but are perfectly safe, endlessly repeatable, always charming, and quite saccharine.' See *Sentimental Twain: Samuel Clemens in the Maze of Moral Philosophy* (Philadelphia: University of Pennsylvania Press, 1994) p. 1. 3. Fred G. See, 'Tom Sawyer and Children's Literature', in Gary Scharnhorst (ed.), *Critical Essays on the Adventures of Tom Sawyer* (New York: G.K. Hall, 1993) p. 179 4. Lee Clark Mitchell, 'Introduction' to *The Adventures of Tom Sawyer*, p. x

a simpler society, when the tensions that marked Twain's own period, and—in more extreme form—our own, did not exist. 'Twain', in Louis J. Budd's words, 'charms millions as the magic flutist of nostalgia for childhood in a simpler, nicer time'.[5]

Such forms of cultural nostalgia generally cover over the fact that authenticity, wholeness, innocence and security retreat endlessly before the search for them. Twain knew this, and, as Cynthia Griffin Wolff points out in referring to the 'darker side' of the novel (the 'ominous air of violence' that suffuses it), 'every one of [the] sentimental evocations' of *Tom Sawyer* as 'exuding the security of childhood-as-it-ought-to-be in small-town America . . . is false to the original'.[6] Twain's reconstruction of community life in a Missouri riverbank town of the 1830s or 1840s ('thirty or forty years ago') is not the simple exercise in antimodernism for which it is so often taken. Rather, the ambiguities and contradictions of the book reveal cultural tensions both of the time of the novel's setting and of its writing.

Tom Sawyer relates both to Twain's American present and its past. It was just one of a spate of 'boy books' written in the period between the end of the Civil War and the early twentieth century, but set in the ante-bellum period. The long period of the genre's popularity testifies, for Marcia Jacobson, 'to the fact that it spoke to persistent and apparently insoluble needs on the part of Americans' in a period of 'massive, disruptive social change'. Jacobson sees the boy book as offering a 'vicarious escape from . . . the culture that produced it'.[7] The vicarious escape offered by Twain's novel, however, is not into a world which differs completely from that of the 1870s. Undoubtedly the social patterns, forms of economic activity and institutional frameworks represented in his fictional St Petersburg are simpler, and allow room for the type of individual freedom of action and movement that would later disappear. The nostalgic quality of the book stems in part from this. But though modernisation increased remarkably in speed and intensity in the post-bellum period, what occurred was a series of developments *within* an existing process, and no sudden transformation. The social critique in *Tom Sawyer* is directed not just at Gilded Age America [approximately the

5. Louis J. Budd, 'Mark Twain as an American Icon', in Forrest G. Robinson (ed.), *The Cambridge Companion to Mark Twain* (Cambridge: Cambridge University Press, 1995) p. 6 6. Cynthia Griffin Wolff, '*The Adventures of Tom Sawyer:* A Nightmare Vision of American Boyhood', *Massachusetts Review*, vol. 21, no. 4 (Winter 1980) pp. 99, 94 7. Marcia Jacobson, *Being a Boy Again: Autobiography and the American Boy Book* (Tuscaloosa: University of Alabama Press, 1994) pp. 4, 7, 13

last three decades of the nineteenth century] but at the conditions of Jacksonian America [approximately 1825–1850] too. The escape that it offers has more to do with the *boy* than the place: one who functions at the margins of the normal social rules and constraints, and who is associated with charisma, heroic individualism and the spirit of play.

But the forms of escape associated with Tom are always, in turn, compromised by pressures toward cultural conformity. There is a peculiar double movement to Twain's text. . . . Tom Sawyer is both a rebellious *and* a socially respectable, even representative, figure. He is given the authority and agency of the free individual *and* made subject to the pressures of a determining environment. Twain both resists and accepts the historical logic of American capitalism; of American cultural life. His novel reveals anxieties about the direction and development of that culture, and the tensions it contains, but also acts to suppress them—acts, to paraphrase Jacobson, to further its dominant ends.[8] In the matter of race relations, in particular, Twain whitewashes the uncomfortable socio-historical facts of American life to massage (however unconsciously) the sensibilities of his audience. The reasons for the novel's enduring popularity may lie not just in its nostalgic appeal, but in its very ambiguities and paradoxes: the way it both resists and accommodates itself to changing American social and economic patterns.[9]. . .

A CHANGING PERCEPTION OF WORK AND PLAY

This is complicated material, and I proceed slowly. At the time Twain wrote *Tom Sawyer*, the cultural perception of the relation between play and work (like that between the savage and the civilised) was rooted in the idea of a child-man divide. This perception was, indeed, already becoming established in the pre-war period of the novel's setting. Michael Oriard looks back to 1830s America to see the start of a pattern that became more evident as the Industrial Revolution advanced: the 'uncomfortable awareness that perhaps leisure, not labor, offered the best possibilities for human fulfilment'. He shows how the

8. Thus Marcia Jacobson's central argument is that the boy book 'could simultaneously be accepted as offering a vicarious escape from and implicit critique of the culture that produced it and as an instrument for furthering the ends of that culture' (*Being a Boy Again*, p. 13). This leads in fruitful directions, as far as *Tom Sawyer* goes, but does not for me quite explain all the complex effects of the book. 9. Lee Clark Mitchell, indeed, discusses the 'mix of contrasts' in *Tom Sawyer* as matching 'the contradictions many have felt about coming of age in American culture', 'Introduction' to *The Adventures of Tom Sawyer*, p. xv.

play impulse was harnessed to the new industrial order as the nineteenth century progressed. Recognising the 'labor/leisure dualism at the heart of industrial capitalism', and its corollary, that 'play embodied a countercultural desire for work-oriented men' in Gilded Age America, Oriard shows how the boy (and girl) book provided a way of containing and disguising such tensions.[10] These books helped to smooth over the divide between labour and leisure in their celebration of 'work and play as two halves of the ideal life', with childhood represented as 'the time for play'. This allowed for the creation of a series of 'idealized figures on whom middle-class America projected its desires and fantasies, but without jeopardising its ultimate commitment to work'.[11]

Twain's book, however, complicates this pattern. For *Tom Sawyer* never quite works as the story of a merely playful boy. Rather, Twain implicates Tom in the business ethic from which childhood, supposedly, provided an alternative and escape. The partial unravelling of the work-play opposition in the whitewashing scene, as the play of childhood overlaps with work, points to the ambiguities in Tom's representation in the novel. He is associated both with 'boyhood's free spirit'[12] and with proto-capitalist attitudes and practices.[13] He is nostalgically linked throughout the novel with adventure, imagination and the escape from the responsible adult world, but also depicted as an entrepreneur, an emergent businessman, finally rewarded by the status, praise and fortune which symbolise complete social acceptance and success. The peculiar double effects here do not add up. The gap between labour and leisure differs from the model Oriard suggests,[14] for Tom is simultaneously both

---

10. Michael Oriard, *Sporting with the Gods: The Rhetoric of Play and Game in American Culture* (Cambridge: Cambridge University Press, 1991) pp. xi, 11, 369, 394. *Tom Sawyer* is a book written about a boy and one primarily directed toward male readers (see for instance the remark on whistling, p. 11). Oriard is particularly interesting on the difference between boy and girl books at this time, and makes the revealing comment that, if play can be linked to such a 'countercultural desire for work-oriented men', then 'work embodied the reformist desire of play-burdened women' (p. 394; and see pp. 394–9). See also Steven Mailloux's valuable essay, 'The Rhetorical Use and Abuse of Fiction: Eating Books in Late Nineteenth-Century America', in Donald E. Pease, *Revisionary Interventions in the American Canon* (Durham, NC: Duke University Press, 1994) especially pp. 140–50. 11. *Sporting with the Gods*, pp. 399, 398 12. John Seelye, 'Introduction' to *The Adventures of Tom Sawyer* (London: Penguin, 1986 [1876]) p. xi 13. My approach, and the terms I use here, are influenced by Scott Michaelsen's unpublished article, 'Tom Sawyer's Capitalisms and the Destructuring of Huck Finn'. My thanks to him for allowing me to make use of it. Other critics, too, refer to this aspect of the novel. See, for example, Lee Clark Mitchell, who says that Tom anticipates many techniques 'we accept today as commonplace business ploys', 'Introduction' to *The Adventures of Tom Sawyer* (World's Classics) p. xiv. 14. Though Oriard's analysis of the novel and especially his insistence on the 'safe' quality of Tom's play is still to the point: *Sporting with the Gods*, p. 401.

playful boy and apprentice businessman. Twain appears, moreover, to criticise capitalist attitudes and values in his description of the methods Tom uses to achieve his profitable ends, and his suggestion of what is being sacrificed in the process. But if ambivalences appear here about the values associated with the world of labour which are, in the boy book, normally covered over, Twain has his own way of (partially) disguising them. The criticism of business values remains implicit rather than overt; suppressed, to considerable degree, by the *confusion* of work and play, by the nostalgic tone of the book, and by Tom's central, and often heroic, role in the success story it enacts. To start to unpack the contradictions in Tom's representation and the divisions in his performance is, though, to suggest the cultural tensions it masks. A strong note of ambiguity concerning his activities runs right the way through the novel.

Tom's first fortune results from his whitewashing scam, which leaves him 'literally rolling in wealth'. If to whitewash is to 'cover up and conceal', Tom conceals rather a lot in the victory he wins at the expense both of Aunt Polly and his friends. Later, when Becky is threatened with punishment following her accidental tearing of the schoolteacher's *Anatomy* book, Tom says that 'girls' faces always tell on them'. Here, he disguises his intentions behind a false face, 'took up his brush and went tranquilly to work' once he decides on his plan to whitewash his friends; to con them out of their possessions. For Jesse Bier is not alone in seeing Tom as a 'con man'.[15] Tom tricks his friends into doing his work for him, and relieves them of their wealth, whatever its form ('twelve marbles . . . a tin soldier . . . a kitten with only one eye') into the bargain. Unearned increment is too modest a term to describe the capital Tom accumulates out of nothing but Aunt Polly's raw materials and his wits alone.

In *Confidence Men and Painted Women: A Study of Middle-class Culture in America, 1830–1870*, Karen Halttunen identifies the figure of the confidence man as standing at 'the

---

15. Quoted in Alan Gribben, '"I Did Wish Tom Sawyer Was There": Boy-Book Elements in *Tom Sawyer* and *Huckleberry Finn*', in Robert Sattelmeyer and J. Donald Crowley (eds), *One Hundred Years of Huckleberry Finn: The Boy, His Book, and American Culture* (Columbia: University of Missouri Press, 1985) p. 149. Forrest Robinson refers to Tom's 'consummate mastery of face' and calls him 'the leading gamesman in St Petersburg'. He also says that 'in winning his way to the top, Tom outwits and exploits every age group and class in the community', *In Bad Faith: The Dynamics of Deception in Mark Twain's America* (Cambridge, Mass: Harvard University Press, 1986), pp. 31, 28–9, 25.

center of anxieties that advice manuals expressed about American youth' in the period. These anxieties focused on the move, on the part of young men in particular, 'far beyond the surveillance of their families, their towns, and their churches' as they responded to ante-bellum social change and sought work 'in the booming cities of industrializing America'. The confidence man, she continues, became a figure representing all that was threatening in 'the growing confusion and anonymity of urban living'. Charisma was likely to replace established social authority in such conditions, and 'fluid self-aggrandisement' easily resulted from the hypocrisy and duplicity—beneath the mask of perfect sincerity—of such trickster figures.[16]

This fearful scenario was already becoming established in the Jacksonian period about which Twain wrote. In one very obvious sense, however, Tom Sawyer cannot be associated with such anxieties, firmly bound as he is to the relatively self-contained small-town world of St Petersburg (referred to variously as both town and village). One might, however, see here both a hint of the fears of that period, and an anxiety about the types of changes (and the figures who would symbolise them) altering America, both before and after the Civil War.[17] For the processes of social transformation in the period were continuous ones. Twain represents Tom not only as a proto-capitalist but as a confidence man into the bargain. In doing so he taps into anxieties not only about business values but about social status too: anxieties first apparent in Jacksonian times but present in more persistent and stronger form in Gilded Age America.[18]. . .

But there are signs of a more fundamental change in the social order here, too. Tom is associated . . . not with a childhood disruption of established authority, but with the establishment of new patterns of social authority and success. Here, in other words (and in contrast to his former role), he actually represents the dominant values of an emergent capitalist culture. The tensions within the book are clear as such a representation clashes with Tom's position as a figure of anti-modernist wish-fulfilment: the playful child who cannot

16. See Karen Halttunen, *Confidence Men and Painted Women: A Study of Middle-class Culture in America, 1830–1870* (New Haven, Conn.: Yale University Press, 1982) pp. 3, 1, 7, 23, 25, 33–4 17. John Carlos Rowe speaks of the intense economic activity on the ante-bellum southwestern frontier as helping 'Jacksonian America enter the modern industrial age', 'Fatal Speculations', p. 141. 18. See too the links Neil Schmitz makes between Jacksonian values and Twain's representations of the Gilded Age in 'Mark Twain, Henry James, and Jacksonian Dreaming', *Criticism*, vol. 27 (Spring 1985) pp. 155–73.

be pinned down by society's fixed routines and disciplines, and who can temporarily escape its authority adventuring on Jackson's Island or Cardiff Hill. . . .

As *Tom Sawyer* ends, Tom's money is out 'at six-per-cent' and his income is 'prodigious'. He is, then, certainly shown as, in some degree, an apprentice version of the 'man-on-the-make' whose charisma, enterprise and eye for the main chance together bring him success. This script addresses (in however veiled a manner) anxieties about social and economic change in the Jacksonian period about which Twain was writing, but also in Gilded Age America too. The social order Twain describes in the novel is one in transition, with (or so it is implied) the introduction of new patterns of wealth based on enterprise[19] rather than birth. The final sequences of *Tom Sawyer* indicate a dramatic change in social and status hierarchies that complements Tom and Huck's new wealth: the two boys earn as much hard cash, in interest on their money, as the minister gets in a good week, and their twelve thousand dollars 'was more than anyone present [at its counting] had ever seen at one time before, though several persons were there who were worth considerable more than that in property'. New ways of measuring wealth, and of determining social hierarchy and authority, are readily apparent here.

NOT NECESSARILY AN ATTACK ON CAPITALISM

This, though, is a lop-sided reading of the novel. Undoubtedly anxieties about money, class and social change, and their effect (both before and after the Civil War) on American culture are evident in *Tom Sawyer*. But it is easy to read the book . . . as about childhood skylarking and adventure, and the escape from the adult world of responsibility and business success, rather than seeing the representation of Tom as a site for social critique. Indeed, to recognise Tom's business side is not necessarily to see Twain as attacking capitalist values; for his enterprise and material gain, both legitimised by the traditional American success ethos, are expected components of the popular genres (adventure and

19. Enterprise and theft continue to stand for one another here. An alternative interpretation would focus on the *difference* between Tom's earlier exploits and the 'finding of gold in the ground' motif. There are parallels here with *Roughing It*: nostalgia for an imaginary time when individual luck, pluck and financial success went hand in hand, prior to the coming of systematised forms of corporate activity and the creation of a wage-earning middle class. The possibility of such variants suggests the ambiguities of the novel.

romance) on which Twain relies. Moreover, though the narrating voice might at times adopt a tone open to ironic interpretation in describing the way Tom accrues wealth, and his accompanying actions, it would be difficult to read the novel (and especially its final sequences) consistently in terms of such a deliberate intent. If the boy book genre generally recalled past cultural vitality and authenticity,[20] then it is Tom's opposition to the 'frowsy hum of study' in the schoolplace, his subversion of day-to-day institutional and social rituals, and his imaginative efforts to escape these boundaries into a world of heroic individualism and romantic adventure which undoubtedly helped (and helps) to account for Tom Sawyer's success. In other words, and again, cultural tensions are both revealed and masked here. Tom is shown both as boy businessman (the child as father of the man) and as romantic rebel at one and the same time. Anxieties about the growth and direction of an entrepreneurial and materialist society are balanced, on one side, by an implied acceptance of its norms, on the other, by a return to an apparently unproblematic ante-bellum world of childhood play.

20. See Marcia Jacobson, *Being a Boy Again*, p. 16.

An Antisocial Revolt

Maxwell Geismar

Tom Sawyer is Twain's satire on the basic values of civilization, according to Maxwell Geismar. He finds the book's appeal is strongest in its wistful, comic parody of adult society founded on power acquisition and manipulation. Geismar, who uses Twain's real name, Sam Clemens, when writing about "the man behind the artist," has written several books on other American authors of the nineteenth and twentieth centuries, including Ernest Hemingway, Edith Wharton, and William Faulkner.

Whether [*Tom Sawyer*] was a children's book for adults, as Clemens first believed, or for children, as it turned out at the time, and not too successfully either, it is certain that when Mark Twain went back to his memories of childhood the deepest preoccupations of his temperament emerged more clearly. If Twain traced his own ancestry to the Garden of Eden in fact, this was an edenic vision of frontier life in which the young hero was both an orphan and a devil. "He's full of the Old Scratch," says Aunt Polly, "but laws-a-me! he is my own dead sister's boy, poor thing, and I ain't got the heart to lash him, somehow." And if there was one thing in the world that Tom Sawyer hated more than anything else, it was *work*. In its underlying satire, this paradise of playtime was also a travesty not merely of American society but of civilization's basic values. It was an outwitting, through art, of the adult world which all "mature" adults could approve of, just as it praised freely the variations of childhood's gangsters, thieves and crooks in its antisocial revolt. In Tom's first battle with the new boy "in the little shabby village of St. Petersburg," Clemens showed up the mixture of cowardice, bluffing, verbal bombast, and chicanery which all the animals indulge in, and only man deplores. In this heavenly arena, too, there were happy slaves and a racial intermingling.

In the opening scene of the novel, the whitewashing of the fence, Tom remembers the company of children at the town pump. "White, mulatto, and Negro boys and girls were always there waiting their turns, resting, trading playthings, quarreling, fighting, skylarking . . ." And we are told that Work consists of whatever a body is *obliged* to do, and Play consists of whatever a body is not obliged to do. While Ben, forsaking his "Mississippi steamboat," takes over the coveted job of whitewashing, Tom, the "retired artist," sits in the shade, dangles his legs, munches his apples and plans "the slaughter of more innocents." By the middle of the afternoon, Tom, a poverty-stricken boy in the morning, is literally "rolling in wealth"—having been given a kite in good repair, a dead rat on a string, twelve marbles, part of a jew's-harp, a piece of blue bottle-glass, a spool cannon, a key that wouldn't unlock anything, a tin soldier, a couple of tadpoles, six firecrackers, a kitten with only one eye . . . Just as Tom's infantine wickedness is cast in the comic mode, so is the parody of the "acquisitive society," or of capitalism's spurious wealth gained by such devilish manipulation and double-talk on the part of the novel's hero.

REAL LOVE

Tom Sawyer is certainly a boyhood entrepreneur of the highest order, and carries over his trickery (and vanity) into the field of adolescent love affairs. But the emotions of real love are centered in the relationship between him and Aunt Polly. And what is curious is the intensity and the *flow* of such affection under the mask of orphanhood and half-brothers (the suffering Sid of the novel) and mother surrogates and missing (dead) fathers. All of Tom's ostentatious moods of guilt, martyrdom, suffering, remorse are designed to attract Aunt Polly's eye and to solicit her attention; here the cunning mockery of love leads into the genuine article. In terms of Aunt Polly's "punishments" too, and of the harsh moral and religious tradition of the frontier, one is reminded of those cannibalistic savages in Melville's *Typee* who worshiped their savage deities—and beat them up when they were angry at them. The chapter on Sunday school is hilarious in *Tom Sawyer*. There is the boy of German parentage (Twain is careful not to say "German boy") who once recited three thousand verses from the Bible without stopping, "but the strain upon his mental faculties was too great, and he was little better than an idiot from that day forth."

A COMIC SENSE OF EVIL

What is apparent in the blissful atmosphere of frontier boyhood in *Tom Sawyer* is that the sense of evil is comic too. The "diabolism" of the hero, however deep this strain ran in Sam Clemens himself, and despite what might come of it later, is itself a form of playful parody; and life is basically innocent and loving. If *Tom Sawyer* is, on one level, a parody of an adult society of power and manipulation, of property and place, of trading and acquisition—the parody itself is divine, is innocent, is wistful and comic. (That is the real secret of the book's lasting appeal.) Beneath all the humor is the deeper rhythm of Sam Clemens' affinity with animal life and a natural sense of pleasure. Monday mornings always found Tom Sawyer miserable "because it began another week's slow suffering in school," and school, like church, is human nature in fetters, in the prison of civilization. Just here we have the advent of Huckleberry Finn, son of the town drunkard, even more idle, lawless, vulgar; and culture hero that he is to all the "respectable children" who are envious of his gaudy outcast condition.

"Huckleberry came and went, at his own free will. He slept on doorsteps in fine weather and in empty hogsheads in wet; he did not have to go to school or to church, or call any being master or obey anybody; he could go fishing or swimming when and where he chose, and stay as long as it suited him; nobody forbade him to fight; he could sit up as late as he pleased; he was always the first boy that went barefoot in the spring and the last to resume leather in the fall; he never had to wash, nor put on clean clothes; he could swear wonderfully. In a word, everything that goes to make life precious that boy had. So thought every harassed, hampered, respectable boy in St. Petersburg . . . Tom hailed the romantic outcast." Thus, in this boyhood idyll of freedom from civilization in a frontier town, we come finally to the symbol of absolute freedom. In this radically democratic antisocial chronicle of youth, we have at the climax the outcast hero who is the antithesis of all ethical, moral, social, worldly, or financial patterns of "maturity," of human "betterment" or success. Even in the comic mode of childhood.

It is from the ignorant Huck also that we get the dominant use of "nigger" in this story, as though already in the reaches of his unconscious Clemens was evolving his parable of Huck's education. Through Huck also we get the sense of that darker stream of Negro superstitiousness, of African witchcraft, of voodoo charms and cures and curses which runs, like a submerged Mississippi current, through the pages of *Tom Sawyer.* . . . Does this classical work of childhood also hinge upon a ridiculous melodrama: the murder of Dr. Robinson by Injun Joe, who blames the murder on his partner in crime, Muff Potter? We realize again that Clemens was supremely careless about the plot structure of his narratives—or supremely confident that any improvised, twisted, shaky narrative structure could be used to convey his own vision of experience . . . and that what counted was not the improbable structure of his tale but what he could do with it. The episodes of calf love between Tom and Becky Thatcher take up more space in the story, too, than they are worth, and Clemens was slightly uneasy in this area of emotions. And the subplot of the boys escaping to the island, while the whole town and their parents and relatives believe they are dead and prepare a mock funeral, has a sadistic undertone which the comedy of the trick barely obscures.

A CHILDHOOD GARDEN OF INNOCENCE

But then there is the description of the first raft scene in these frontier idylls. Clemens' evocation of the womb theme, or of the (lost!) plenary state of man, or of that childhood garden of innocence which is man's deepest myth, is done so naturally, surely, accurately. There is the water fighting of the naked boys, not altogether in accordance with the Victorian proprieties, and the sumptuous island breakfasts of fish and bacon while these social exiles loaf and contemplate their souls. There are the brilliant passages on frontier education and the "moral and religious mind" (partly reminiscent of Edward Eggleston's *The Hoosier Schoolmaster,* published some five years earlier). There are those pages in *Tom Sawyer* where Clemens indulged himself with some of his satire on school compositions, schoolchildren, and schoolmasters—and on provincial poetry:

> And cold must be mine eyes, and heart, and tete,
> When, dear Alabama! they turn cold on thee!

In these Twainish notes from an older world, recalling the vanished democracy of the raw western towns in the mid–nineteenth century, before the Civil War and before the establishment of the great American fortunes which changed the whole texture of American life, we realize that the poor, the idle, the vagrants are much more prominent in a village life which has not yet been altogether converted to the rationale of work, social respectability, and material success. The boys pay a visit to the innocent Muff Potter at the town jail, where he is lodged without guards, to bring him tobacco and matches. And indeed, as in his attack on Ben Franklin in *Sketches New and Old*, Clemens makes this point very specifically. "Huck was willing. Huck was always willing to take a hand in any enterprise that offered entertainment and required no capital, for he had troublesome superabundance of that sort of time which is *not* money." You might say that Clemens was the spokesman for that central line of American writers who were at variance from the outset with the materialistic hypocrisy of Franklin.

The end of this childhood classic revolves upon the melodrama of the nightmare vigil of Tom and Becky lost in the island cave—and the "happy ending" of Tom and Huck dividing up the cash loot of twelve thousand dollars which they have discovered in the cave. A happy ending of easy money which is apparently the complete antithesis of the central vision of *Tom Sawyer*, until we realize that Mark Twain was just as adroit as Henry James, say, in the use of literary decoys. For Huck was now rich, and being "educated" into civilized ways by the Widow Douglas.

"He had to go to church; he had to talk so properly that speech was become insipid in his mouth; whither soever he turned, the bars and shackles of civilization shut him in and bound him hand and foot." And he can't stand the process and throws it all over. "Don't talk about it, Tom. I've tried it, and it don't work, it don't work, Tom. It ain't for me; I ain't used to it. The widder's good to me, and friendly; but I can't stand them ways . . . Tom, I wouldn't ever got into all this trouble if it hadn't 'a' been for that money; now you just take my sheer of it along with your'n, and gimme a ten-center sometimes—not many times, becuz I don't give a dern for a thing 'thout it's tollable hard to git—and you go and beg off for me with the widder." Or at least Huck wants to throw it all over, since the novel ends on an ambiguous note. . . .

Our adult strivings appear to be as ludicrous as they really are: mature achievement is a satiric joke. And here all the low, base, and sordid—or even evil—emotions can be openly described for what they are, since in this childhood context they are at the same time not "serious." This is Satan playing in the garden of innocence. And this "make-believe" world of infancy and childhood, of the primitive emotions, even of the animal life that Clemens described so intimately, is in fact . . . a classic source of man's dreams, his psychology, his deep nostalgia, his myths, his art. Before the Fall, in this world of boyhood yearning, while "adventure," "glory," "fame" are primary things, sin is not sin, evil is not evil, cupidity is not cupidity nor is corruption corruption, and death is not yet death. The heroics and villainies of human nature are revealed more clearly just because their whole context and weight has been shifted in the "comedy" scene of childhood innocence; while all of human pretense could be stripped away by the unblinking gaze of childhood candor. This is mock heroics, mock villainy, mock passion, mock pride, and mock despair, in a world of poetic mockery.

A Vacation for Everyone

George P. Elliott

In *Tom Sawyer*, Twain offers both a vacation into boyhood for the reader, and a vacation from many of life's perplexities for the hero. Barnard College professor George P. Elliott, who has written poetry, short stories, and essays, notes Twain's theme as a delightful vacation from reality. The pleasure extends to the reader, who is allowed respite from literary structure and internal coherence in a story that is more dream than message.

Everything about *Tom Sawyer* is turned into a kind of vacationing—even going to school. The one main activity of Mr. Dobbins' school, studying, is scarcely noticeable in the atmosphere of pranks, courtship, and swapping. Besides, the weather of the book is absolutely subversive of school: hot and lazy swimming weather; summertime and hooky; the weather for natural impulse, with Calvinistic thunderstorms punishing along from time to time. Punishment cannot be escaped even on a vacation into boyhood; after all, boyhood is still in this world, and Mark Twain was trained to see stern, arbitrary punishment as being in the nature of things. Even Tom's most enviable friend, Huck Finn, who is on chronic holiday from schoolmasters, Sunday-school teachers, mothers, and aunts, has a father once in a while and knows the Law when it whacks him. But the main punisher in the book, Aunt Polly—who punishes because she has to, as Tom well understands—never resists his love, never resists loving him. Surely a dreamy state of affairs.

AN ESCAPE FROM TROUBLES

Vacations are *from*. Consider some of the perplexities (and also, it must be confessed, splendors) which *Tom Sawyer* takes us from.

Sex: In St. Petersburg love even between the sexes is scarcely perturbed by desire, and knowledge is of the anatomy-book

Afterword to *The Adventures of Tom Sawyer*, by George P. Elliott (New York: Signet, 1959). Copyright © 1959 by the New American Library of World Literature, Inc.

kind. Work: the only job with which Tom is punished he turns into a famous game of whitewashing. Tedium: from the strait *longueurs* of childhood and of respectability we are saved by tricks and dangers and natural impulses. Money: the boy's medium of exchange is barter; the only adults devoted to getting money are stark villains; there's a box of gold coins at the end of this rainbow. Responsibility: Huck *has* none, the Model Boy is the object of loathing, and in full consciousness Tom chooses to wound his aunt severely for the sake of a practical joke.

Sex, work, tedium, money—those are fine troubles to get away from; but responsibility is a more ticklish matter. Maybe the Missouri-Presbyterian code of conscience was indeed a bad one, and certainly it is pleasant to play on a summertime island when no one knows you are there; but gratuitous cruelty costs more than playing hooky is worth. To be sure, the heavens thunder on them, and Tom repents, is punished, and is forgiven. But the storm leaves nothing behind; Tom has learned nothing; these episodes are memory-proof.

For finally Mark Twain was not serious in this book. The writer, too, vacationed. Most of the time his style, at once indolent and vigorous, is harmonious with the tone of the happenings. But sometimes he editorializes, as when he spends a paragraph lambasting the women who petitioned for a pardon for Injun Joe, and this editorializing we accept because it does little harm. Sometimes the melodrama is nothing but blood-and-thunder, "'Now the cussed thing's ready, Sawbones, and you'll just out with another five, or here she stays,'" and this keeps the danger from being real so we don't object. And sometimes he speaks to the reader about his characters and their plight in ways that are hard to enjoy even on vacation: "But the elastic heart of youth cannot be compressed into one constrained shape long at a time." Furthermore, he felt under no obligation to make the book cohere very tightly; there is no plot, there are no real themes, there is a certain moral evasiveness, not even the author's style is completely consistent. Yet if one doesn't ask too much of it, surely the book holds together quite well enough to justify its long and splendid success in the world.

AN ESCAPE TO DELIGHT

For vacations are also *to*. And this book offers a small world of delights to anyone who is willing to unbuckle his strictures for a while.

ALWAYS PLAY, NEVER WORK

In this excerpt from his Autobiography, *a section written in 1908, Twain claimed that he hadn't done a lick of work since 1866—and what he had done before then, he had only done reluctantly.*

From the time that my father died, March 24, 1847, when I was past eleven years old, until the end of 1856, or the first days of 1857, I worked—not diligently, not willingly, but fretfully, lazily, repiningly, complainingly, disgustedly, and always shirking the work when I was not watched. The statistics show that I was a worker during about ten years. I am approaching seventy-three and I believe I have never done any work since—unless I may call two or three years of lazy effort as reporter on the Pacific Coast by that large and honorable name—and so I think I am substantially right in saying that when I escaped from the printing office fifty or fifty-one years ago I ceased to be a worker and ceased permanently.

Piloting on the Mississippi River was not work to me; it was play—delightful play, vigorous play, adventurous play—and I loved it; silver mining in the Humboldt Mountains was play, only play, because I did not do any of the work; my pleasant comrades did it and I sat by and admired; my silver mining in Esmeralda was not work, for Higbie and Robert Howland did it and again I sat by and admired. I accepted a job of shoveling tailings in a quartz mill there, and that was really work and I had to do it myself, but I retired from that industry at the end of two weeks, and not only with my own approval but with the approval of the people who paid the wages. These mining experiences occupied ten months and came to an end toward the close of September, 1862.

I then became a reporter in Virginia City, Nevada, and later in San Francisco, and after something more than two years of this salaried indolence I retired from my position on the *Morning Call*, by solicitation. Solicitation of the proprietor. Then I acted as San Franciscan correspondent of the Virginia City *Enterprise* for two or three months; next I spent three months in pocket-mining at Jackass Gulch with the Gillis boys; then I went to the Sandwich Islands and corresponded thence for the Sacramento *Union* five or six months; in October, 1866, I broke out as a lecturer, and from that day to this I have always been able to gain my living without doing any work; for the writing of books and magazine matter was always play, not work. I enjoyed it; it was merely billiards to me.

The Autobiography of Mark Twain, edited by Charles Neider. New York: Harper, 1959.

Not the least of these delights is getting to know Mark Twain himself, listening to his voice. For example, his invective against the petitioneresses has nothing to do with any of the actions, themes, or characters of the book, but it is great fun in itself and it does not go on too long; furthermore, it is spoken in the voice of a popular entertainer who knows not only how to tell tall tales and take us back into boyhood but also how to exaggerate his own occasional anger into uproar. "Injun Joe was believed to have killed five citizens of the village, but what of that? If he had been Satan himself there would have been plenty of weaklings ready to scribble their names to a pardon petition, and drip a tear on it from their permanently impaired and leaky waterworks." Again and again as the book goes along, we enjoy a pleasure of that sort which is possible only when we feel ourselves relaxed in the hands of a master: Schnabel playing Beethoven, Gielgud as Lear, Louis Armstrong, the Dr. Johnson of Boswell's *Life.* When Tom sets out to woo Becky, we know without thinking about it that Mark Twain will take us safely through stratagems and reversals to success at last; and surely we feel a simple and adequate (and grateful) satisfaction when Tom wins Becky in Chapter XX by sacrificing himself and in Chapter XXXII pluckily saves her from death. We do not enter the book so far—at least adults are not likely to do it—as to forget that quirky old spellbinder who knew just how to do what he was doing.

The unpretentiousness of *Tom Sawyer*—that is a great pleasure, perhaps especially great for a literary reader nowadays. Mark Twain in his shirtsleeves was utterly unpretentious and in fact devoted a good deal of his energy to satirizing pretension. (When he put on the Robe of Literature, as in *Personal Recollections of Joan of Arc* which he was known to speak of as his best book, he could be pretty intolerable himself in the way of pretentiousness.) But in *Tom Sawyer*, things are what they seem and mostly they seem like fun. The characters are not symbolic of richly murky meanings; they are types from comedy and melodrama. Each episode is self-contained; one never has a sense of parable, of message. And when Mark Twain draws a moral it is apt to be of the homespun variety: "He had discovered a great law of human action, without knowing it—namely, that in order to make a man or boy covet a thing, it is only necessary to make the thing difficult to obtain." The product of such a statement is less wisdom than reassurance and a comfortable lack of tension. Mark Twain knew this well enough; he knew that ordinary people like old saws; he liked making up aphorisms (he wrote hundreds of them). With part of himself he had a folksy regard for his own adages, but with another part he knew better. The sentence following the one just quoted reads: "If he had been a great and wise philosopher, like the writer of this book, he would now have comprehended that Work consists of whatever a body is *obliged* to do and that Play consists of whatever a body is not obliged to do."

There is another kind of meaning or significance which literary people have been made hypersensitive to—not the message (heaven forbid!) but the structure, the irony, the ambiguities, the internal coherence, of a book. Well, *Tom Sawyer* has about as little structure as message, and what a holiday *that* is for a literary reader. As for irony, the second sentence quoted above has plenty of irony—about ten inches broad, by my ruler, and a quarter of an inch deep. The main ambiguity I noticed was that the boys and the reader know for half a dozen chapters that the supposedly deaf-and-dumb Spaniard is really Injun Joe whereas the rest of the village does not know it; but since nothing is made of this except to keep the boys and the reader in suspense, since a seven-year-old reader can appreciate it as much as an adult and would no doubt enjoy it more, since it does not "resonate" either in the book or in the reader or anywhere else, I suspect that it is not the sort of irony to fatten the critical intellect on. Praise be.

THE DREAM OF BOYHOOD

The main delight of the book, to be sure, is the dream of boyhood into which we are released by it. "Most of the adventures recorded in this book really occurred," says The Author, fooling no one. Most of the events of a dream may really have occurred too, but not so fast, not in the same order, in different surroundings, with many accompanying events dropped by the way. For instance, a couple of boys of Sam Clemens' acquaintance might actually have witnessed a murder, they might have been afraid to testify to the identity of the true culprit, and one of them might have finally spoken out and saved an innocent man. But by the time these events have been attached to the persons of Tom,

Huck, Injun Joe, and Muff Potter—have been interspersed with other events intrinsically quite unimportant yet similarly treated—have been highlighted, buffooned, typified, and tall-taled—have been recounted in such and such a tone of voice—by that time no reader cares where Mark Twain got the idea for the episode. For what matters in it is that the fear is never presented as too great for the boys to handle, the conflict in Tom's conscience is painful and finds release, and honor is bestowed on him with a lavish hand. It is a dreamlike boyish marvel that Injun Joe shows up again in disguise; the real motive for this reappearance—like the reason for Tom's catching a glimpse of him later in the cave—is Mark Twain's need for a convenient way to generate more scary situations. Injun Joe's depravity is satisfactorily explained by his race, he reappears in the town where he is wanted for murder, by a sort of divinely retributive accident he dies with suitable horribleness: this is not Sam Clemens' boyhood in Hannibal but a fine vacationing country in Mark Twain's mind.

Part of The Author's intention was, overtly, nostalgia: "... for part of my plan has been to try to pleasantly remind adults of what they once were themselves." He refers to his characters as children when he is seeing them from a certain, nostalgic distance, but by their proper names when he has imagined himself back into that land of hooky and justice. A child reading the book pays little attention to the parts written from an adult's point of view and sees adventures rendered as adventures ought to be. An adult must share Mark Twain's nostalgia, for the book is a little like Jackson's Island in that it's a fine place to play in naked innocence if you don't stay too long. For us now, there is a special nostalgia, for us "jung and easily freudened." This is a nostalgia for a simpler conception of childhood, one which has pretty well disappeared, at least among the even partially educated. But how peaceful and easy it is to enjoy a story in which a boy and girl can wander for three days in a cave with nothing more subtle on their minds (or on yours, reading) than cold, hunger, darkness, loneliness, pitfalls, and a desperado who would kill them if he came upon them. It's been a long time. . . .

CHRONOLOGY

For names and dates of more of Twain's works, see "Works by Mark Twain."

1835
November 30—Samuel Langhorne Clemens (who will become Mark Twain) is born in Florida, Missouri.

1838
Frederick Douglass escapes from slavery. Race riots and lynchings have been increasing for three years. The Underground Railroad, which helps slaves escape and tries to protect them from violent pursuers, is established.

1839
The Clemens family moves to Hannibal, Missouri, on the Mississippi River.

1842
British author Charles Dickens tours the United States, crusading for international copyright laws and attacking the institution of slavery.

1843
Sojourner Truth, a freed slave who saw most of her thirteen children sold as slaves, speaks out against slavery around the country.

1845
Editor John L. O'Sullivan writes that the nation has a "Manifest Destiny"—that it is the will of God that the United States expand and control the entire North American continent.

1847
March—Sam's father, John Marshall Clemens, dies.

1848
Sam is apprenticed to the Hannibal *Courier* to learn the newspaper trade. Gold is discovered near Sutter's Mill in California; gold rush begins. Political and social revolutions and rebellions sweep Europe.

1850

September—Orion Clemens, Sam's brother, begins publishing the weekly Hannibal *Western Union.* In the same month, Congress adopts the Compromise of 1850 in an attempt to prevent the dissolution of the Union over the issue of slavery.

1851

January—Sam begins working on the *Western Union.*

1852

Harriet Beecher Stowe's *Uncle Tom's Cabin* is published. On July 4, Frederick Douglass states that Negroes should not celebrate Independence Day, since so many of them are slaves. Daniel Webster and Henry Clay, who helped hold the Union together while clashing on most other issues, both die this year.

1854

Abraham Lincoln calls for the gradual emancipation of slaves; "No man is good enough to govern another man without that other's consent," he asserts.

1855

Walt Whitman pays to have his book *Leaves of Grass* printed, and sets ten of its ninety-five pages into type himself.

1856

October 18—Sam's first letter signed "Thomas Jefferson Snodgrass" appears in the Keokuk, Iowa, *Daily Post.*

1857

Overspeculation in railroads and real estate leads to national financial panic. Sam begins training as a riverboat pilot.

1858

June 13—The steamer *Philadelphia* explodes; victims include Sam's brother Henry, who dies six days later.

1859

April 9—Sam Clemens receives his pilot's license.

June—The Comstock silver lode is discovered in Nevada.

1860

November 6—Abraham Lincoln is elected president.

December 20—South Carolina votes to secede from the Union.

1861

January 21–March 30—Sam's "Quintus Curtius Snodgrass" letters are published in the New Orleans *Crescent.*

February 28—The Nevada Territory (known then as the Washoe) is created from land taken from Mexico.

April 14—Fort Sumter, South Carolina, is captured by Confederate forces.

April 15—Lincoln declares a state of "insurrection." The American Civil War begins.

June—Ten more states have seceded to join South Carolina in the Confederacy.

June—Sam sees brief service with the Confederate Marion's Rangers ("The Campaign That Failed").

July—Sam and Orion go to Carson City, Nevada, where Orion is to take up his post as the secretary of the Nevada Territory.

1862

February–July—Sam's "Josh" letters are published in the Virginia City *Territorial Enterprise.*

August—Sam joins the Enterprise staff.

1863

January 1—Lincoln signs the Emancipation Proclamation.

February 3—Sam first uses "Mark Twain" byline.

November 20—Lincoln delivers the Gettysburg Address.

1864

May—Twain leaves Virginia City for San Francisco.

October 31—Nevada becomes a state; cynics suggest that the timing—just before the November presidential election—is intended to help Lincoln's chances for reelection.

1865

March 4—Lincoln is sworn in for his second term as president.

April 9—Confederate general Robert E. Lee surrenders to Union general Ulysses S. Grant at Appomattox, Virginia, bringing the Civil War to an end.

April 14—Lincoln is assassinated.

November 18—"The Celebrated Jumping Frog of Calaveras County" is printed in the New York *Saturday Press.* Relief at the end of the war has many Americans looking for light-hearted fare; the "Frog" is an immediate success.

1866

Twain spends four months in the Sandwich Islands (Hawaii). On his return to San Francisco he begins giving lectures, earning enough by December to pay for his passage to New York.

1867

May—*The Celebrated Jumping Frog of Calaveras County and Other Sketches* is published.

June 8—As travel correspondent for the San Francisco *Alta California*, Twain sails on the *Quaker City* for a tour of the Mediterranean and the Holy Land. This tour will become the basis of *The Innocents Abroad.*

December 27—Twain meets Olivia ("Livy") Langdon.

1869

February 4—Sam becomes engaged to Livy.

1870

February 2—Sam marries Livy.

November 7—Their first child, Langdon Clemens, is born.

1872

March 19—Olivia Susan (Susy) Clemens is born.

June 2—Langdon Clemens (Sam and Livy's only son) dies.

1873

December—*The Gilded Age* is published. The title of this tale of rampant greed and financial chicanery will be used to describe the entire period from 1870 to 1898.

1874

June 8—Clara Clemens is born.

1880

July 26—Jean Clemens is born.

1884

Twain campaigns for Grover Cleveland for president.

1885

Fall—Twain publishes the memoirs of Ulysses S. Grant.

1890

Twain begins investing in the Paige typesetting machine.

1891

March 4—The International Copyright Act Twain and Dickens lobbied for is passed, protecting foreign authors from piracy at the hands of American publishers. (Twain, who has suffered piracy from publishers around the world, hopes other countries will follow suit.)

1892

King Leopold II of Belgium, who rules the Congo Free State, imposes forced labor on the natives. His personal rule of the region will become so scandalous that on October 18, 1908, the Belgian parliament will take over the country, renaming it the Belgian Congo (today called Zaire).

1893

A stock-market crash in June leads to a national financial panic; by the end of the year, the country is in what is being called the worst depression in its history.

July 12—Frederick Jackson Turner declares that the American "frontier has gone, and with it has closed the first period of American history."

1894

April 18—With the failure of his publishing company and other financial difficulties, Twain is bankrupt.

June—Coal miners end a bloody two-month strike, undertaken to protest wage cuts and dangerous working conditions. Unrest in the coal industry has decimated Livy's income from coal stocks.

1895

July—Twain begins world lecture tour to pay off debts.

1896

August 18—Susy Clemens dies.

1898

The Twains' last debts are paid off in late 1898 or early 1899. In winning the Spanish-American War, the United States establishes itself as a world power. The Anti-Imperialist League objects to the growing drive to claim American colonies. Twain, reformer Jane Addams, philosopher William James, industrialist Andrew Carnegie, labor leader Samuel Gompers, and thirty thousand other members of the league object to U.S. conquests to build an empire.

1901

February—*To the Person Sitting in Darkness* is published (the publisher is the Anti-Imperialist League of New York).

1904

June 5—Livy Clemens dies.

1905

King Leopold's Soliloquy: A Defense of His Congo Rule, about Leopold II's ill-treatment of his subjects in the Congo (see 1892 above), is published.

1909

December 24—Jean Clemens dies.

1910

April 21—Mark Twain dies.

FOR FURTHER RESEARCH

BIOGRAPHIES

Guy Cardwell, *The Man Who Was Mark Twain*. New Haven, CT: Yale University Press, 1991.

Clara Clemens, *My Father, Mark Twain*. New York: Harper & Brothers, 1931.

Cyril Clemens, *Young Sam Clemens*. Portland, ME: Leon Tebbetts, 1942.

Susy Clemens, *Papa: An Intimate Biography of Mark Twain*. Garden City, NY: Doubleday, 1985.

Clinton Cox, *Mark Twain: America's Humorist, Dreamer, Prophet*. New York: Scholastic, 1995.

Everett Emerson, *The Authentic Mark Twain: A Literary Biography of Samuel Clemens*. Philadelphia: University of Pennsylvania Press, 1984.

John D. Evans, *A* Tom Sawyer *Companion: An Autobiographical Guided Tour with Mark Twain*. Lanham, MD: University Press of America, 1993.

Delancey Ferguson, *Mark Twain, Man and Legend*. New York: Russell and Russell, 1965.

Andrew Jay Hoffman, *Inventing Mark Twain: The Lives of Samuel Langhorne Clemens*. New York: William Morrow, 1997.

William Dean Howells, *My Mark Twain: Reminiscences and Criticisms*. New York: Harper & Brothers, 1910.

Justin Kaplan, *Mark Twain and His World*. New York: Simon and Schuster, 1974.

———, *Mr. Clemens and Mark Twain: A Biography*. New York: Simon and Schuster, 1966.

John Lauber, *The Inventions of Mark Twain*. New York: Hill and Wang, 1990.

———, *The Making of Mark Twain: A Biography*. New York: American Heritage Press, 1985.

Stephen Butler Leacock, *Mark Twain*. New York: Haskell House, 1974.

Edgar Lee Masters, *Mark Twain: A Portrait*. New York: Scribner's, 1938.

Charles Nieder, *Mark Twain*. New York: Horizon, 1967.

Albert Bigelow Paine, *Mark Twain: A Biography. The Personal and Literary Life of Samuel Langhorne Clemens*. 3 vols. New York: Harper & Brothers, 1912.

George Sanderlin, *Mark Twain: As Others Saw Him*. New York: Coward, McCann & Geoghegan, 1978.

Henry Nash Smith, *Mark Twain: The Development of a Writer*. Cambridge, MA: Harvard University Press, 1962.

Jeffrey Steinbrink, *Getting to Be Mark Twain*. Berkeley and Los Angeles: University of California Press, 1991.

Edward Wagenknecht, *Mark Twain: The Man and His Work*. New Haven, CT: Yale University Press, 1935.

Dixon Wecter, *Sam Clemens of Hannibal*. Boston: Houghton Mifflin, 1952.

ANALYSIS AND CRITICISM

John E. Bassett, *"A Heart of Ideality in My Realism" and Other Essays on Howells and Twain*. West Cornwall, CT: Locust Hill Press, 1991.

Walter Blair, "On the Structure of *Tom Sawyer*," *Modern Philology*, August 1939.

Edgar J. Burde, "Slavery and the Boys: *Tom Sawyer* and the Germ of *Huck Finn*," *American Literary Realism 1870–1910*, Fall, 1991.

Neil Campbell, "The 'Seductive Outside' and the 'Sacred Precincts': Boundaries and Transgressions in *The Adventures of Tom Sawyer*," *Children's Literature in Education*, vol. 25, no. 2, 1994.

James M. Cox, *Mark Twain: The Fate of Humor*. Princeton, NJ: Princeton University Press, 1966.

Judith Fetterley, "The Sanctioned Rebel," *Studies in the Novel*, Fall 1971.

Robert Giddings, ed., *Mark Twain: A Sumptuous Variety*. Totowa, NJ: Barnes & Noble Books, 1985.

Susan K. Harris, *Mark Twain's Escape from Time: A Study in Patterns and Images*. Columbia: University of Missouri Press, 1982.

Hamlin Hill, "The Composition and the Structure of *Tom Sawyer*," in *On Mark Twain: The Best from American Literature*, eds. Louis J. Budd and Edwin H. Cady. Durham, NC: Duke University Press, 1987.

Elmo Howell, "In Defense of Tom Sawyer," *Mark Twain Journal*, Winter, 1970.

D.M. McKeithan, *Court Trials in Mark Twain and Other Essays*. The Hague, Netherlands: Martinus Nijhoff, 1958.

Franklin R. Rogers, *Mark Twain's Burlesque Patterns, As Seen in the Novels and Narratives 1855–1885*. Dallas: Southern Methodist University Press, 1960.

John Seelye, "What's in a Name: Sounding the Depths of *Tom Sawyer*," *Sewanee Review*, Summer 1982.

Roberty Tracy, "Myth and Reality in *The Adventures of Tom Sawyer*," *Southern Review*, Spring 1968.

Virginia Wexman, "The Role of Structure in *Tom Sawyer* and *Huckleberry Finn*," *American Literary Realism 1870–1910*, Winter 1973.

LITERARY OR HISTORICAL BACKGROUND

Walter Blair, ed., *Mark Twain's Hannibal, Huck, and Tom.* Berkeley and Los Angeles: University of California Press, 1969.

Carl Bode, ed., *American Life in the 1840s*. Garden City, NY: Anchor, 1967.

John M. Dobson, *Politics in the Gilded Age*. New York: Praeger, 1972.

Frank Otto Gattell and John M. McFaul, eds., *Jacksonian America, 1815–1840*. Englewood Cliffs, NJ: Prentice-Hall, 1970.

Arthur M. Schlesinger Jr., *The Age of Jackson*. Boston: Little, Brown, 1953.

THE WORLD WIDE WEB

Websites are notoriously ephemeral, but new information is posted often, so a good search engine will help track down the latest postings. At this writing, interesting information about Twain and *Tom Sawyer* can be found at these websites:

- **http://etext.lib.virginia.edu/twain** (posted by the Electronic Text Center at the University of Virginia, and likely to remain available)
- **http://web.mit.edu/linguistics/www/forum/twainweb.html** (includes archives of messages posted to the Mark Twain Forum)
- **http://marktwain.miningco.com** (includes links to electronic texts, reviews, and a variety of useful information)

WORKS BY MARK TWAIN

Since many volumes and many different editions and combinations of Mark Twain's work have been made available over the years (and previously unpublished material still appears occasionally), the following is not a complete listing. Short stories and essays are generally included only when they have been collected into books; dates are for first U.S. publication.

The Celebrated Jumping Frog of Calaveras County and Other Sketches (1867)

The Innocents Abroad, or The New Pilgrims' Progress (1869)

Mark Twain's (Burlesque) Autobiography and First Romance (1871)

Roughing It (1872)

The Gilded Age: A Tale of To-day (with Charles Dudley Warner) (1873)

Mark Twain's Sketches (1874)

Sketches, New and Old (1875)

The Adventures of Tom Sawyer (1876)

Ah Sin (with Bret Harte) (1877)

A True Story and the Recent Carnival of Crime (The Facts Concerning the Recent Carnival of Crime in Connecticut) (1877)

Punch, Brothers, Punch! and Other Sketches (1877)

A Tramp Abroad (1880)

"1601" or Conversation at the Social Fireside as It Was in the Time of the Tudors (1880)

The Prince and the Pauper (1882)

The Stolen White Elephant, Etc. (1882)

Life on the Mississippi (1883)

The Adventures of Huckleberry Finn (Tom Sawyer's Comrade) (1885)

Mark Twain's Library of Humor. Edited by Samuel Langhorne Clemens, William Dean Howells, and Charles Hopkins Clark. (Contains works by Twain, "Anonymous," and forty-six other authors) (1888)

A Connecticut Yankee in King Arthur's Court (1889)

The Man That Corrupted Hadleyburg (1890)

The American Claimant (1892)

Merry Tales (1892)

The £1,000,000 Bank-note and Other New Stories (1893)

The Niagara Book (by W.D. Howells, Mark Twain, Prof. Nathaniel S. Shaler, and others) (1893)

The Tragedy of Pudd'nhead Wilson and the Comedy of Those Extraordinary Twins (by 1899 called *Pudd'nhead*

Wilson and Those Extraordinary Twins) (1894)

Tom Sawyer Abroad ("by Huck Finn, edited by Mark Twain") (1894)

The Personal Recollections of Joan of Arc (1896)

Tom Sawyer Abroad, Tom Sawyer Detective, and Other Stories (1896)

How to Tell a Story and Other Essays (1897)

Following the Equator (1897)

The Man That Corrupted Hadleyburg and Other Stories and Essays (1900)

To the Person Sitting in Darkness (1901)

A Double Barrelled Detective Story (1902)

My Debut as a Literary Person with Other Essays and Stories (1903)

The Jumping Frog in English, Then in French, Then Clawed Back into a Civilized Language Once More by Patient Unremunerated Toil (1903)

Extracts from Adam's Diary, Translated from the Original MS (1904)

A Dog's Tale (1904)

King Leopold's Soliloquy: A Defense of His Congo Rule (1905)

Editorial Wild Oats (1905)

Eve's Diary, Translated from the Original MS (1906)

What Is Man? (1906)

The $30,000 Bequest and Other Stories (1906)

Christian Science (1907)

A Horse's Tale (1907)

Extract from Captain Stormfield's Visit to Heaven (1909)

Is Shakespeare Dead? From My Autobiography (1909)

PUBLISHED POSTHUMOUSLY

Mark Twain's Speeches. Compiled by F.A. Nast. Introduction by W.D. Howells. (1910)

Death Disk (1915)

The Mysterious Stranger (1916)

Mark Twain's Letters. Edited by Albert Bigelow Paine. (1917)

Who Was Sarah Findlay? With a Suggested Solution of the Mystery by J.M. Barrie (1917)

The Curious Republic of Gondour and Other Whimsical Sketches (by Samuel L. Clemens) (1919)

Mark Twain, Able Yachtsman, Interviews Himself on Why Lipton Failed to Lift the Cup (1920)

The Writings of Mark Twain. 37 vols. Edited by Albert Bigelow Paine. (Includes *Mark Twain's Autobiography*, 2 vols., 1924.) (1922–1925)

The Adventures of Thomas Jefferson Snodgrass. Edited by Charles Honce. (1928)

A Champagne Cocktail and a Catastrophe: Two Acting Charades (1930)

Mark Twain's Notebook. Edited by Albert Bigelow Paine. (1935)

Letters from the Sandwich Islands Written for the Sacramento Union *by Mark Twain.* Edited by G. Ezra Dane. (1938)

Mark Twain in Eruption: Hitherto Unpublished Pages About Men and Events. Edited by Bernard De Voto. (1940)

Mark Twain's Travels with Mr. Brown. Edited by G. Ezra Dane. (1940)

Mark Twain's Letters to Will Bowen: "My First & Oldest & Dearest Friend." Edited by Theodore Hornberger. (1941)

Mark Twain's Letters in the Muscatine Journal. Edited by Edgar M. Branch. (1942)

The Letters of Quintus Curtius Snodgrass (1946)

The Love Letters of Mark Twain. Edited by Dixon Wecter. (1949)

Mark Twain to Mrs. Fairbanks. Edited by Dixon Wecter. (1949)

Mark Twain to Uncle Remus. (Joel Chandler Harris) Edited by Thomas H. English. (1953)

Mark Twain of the Enterprise. Edited by Henry Nash Smith with Frederick Anderson. (1957)

The Autobiography of Mark Twain. Edited by Charles Neider. (Quotations from the *Autobiography* in the present work were taken from this version.) (1959)

Mark Twain–Howells Letters: The Correspondence of Samuel L. Clemens and William Dean Howells, 1872–1910. 2 vols. Edited by Henry Nash Smith and William M. Gibson. (Cover says "1869–1910.") (1960)

Mark Twain's Letters to Mary. Edited by Lewis Leary. (1961)

Letters from the Earth. Edited by Bernard De Voto. (1962)

Early Tales and Sketches, vol. 1 (1851–1864). Edited by Edgar Marquess Branch and Robert H. First with Harriet Elinor Smith. (1979)

The Outrageous Mark Twain: Some Lesser-Known but Extra-ordinary Works, with "Reflections on Religion" Now in Book Form for the First Time. Edited by Charles Neider. (1987)

Mark Twain's Aquarium: The Samuel Clemens Angelfish Correspondence, 1905–1910. Edited by John Cooley. (1991)

The Adventures of Huckleberry Finn. With new text; foreword and addendum by Victor Doyno, introduction by Justin Kaplan. Includes omissions and variations from the recently discovered first half of Twain's manuscript. (1996)

INDEX